THE SOCIALIST POEMS OF
HUGH MACDIARMID

by the same author

The Hugh MacDiarmid Anthology
edited by
Michael Grieve and Alexander Scott

THE SOCIALIST POEMS OF
HUGH MACDIARMID

edited by

T.S.LAW and THURSO BERWICK

ROUTLEDGE & KEGAN PAUL

London, Henley and Boston

*This collection
first published in 1978
by Routledge & Kegan Paul Ltd
39 Store Street,
London WC1E 7DD,
Broadway House,
Newtown Road,
Henley-on-Thames,
Oxon RG9 1EN and
9 Park Street,
Boston, Mass. 02108, USA
Set in Century by Pentagon Printing Group,
Soho Square, London W1
and printed in Great Britain by
Thomson Litho Ltd, East Kilbride*

British Library Cataloguing in Publication Data

MacDiarmid, Hugh, b.1892

*The socialist poems of Hugh MacDiarmid.
I.Title
821'.9'12 PR6013.R735A17 77-30727*

ISBN 0 7100 8914 7

SOURCES

The poems in this volume were taken from the following works:
The Battle Continues (1957), no. 57; *To Circumjack Cencrastus* (1930), nos 5, 6, 10, 22; *A Clyack Sheaf* (1969), nos 17, 28, 56, 61; *Collected Poems* (1962), nos 37, 40, 62; *A Drunk Man Looks at the Thistle* (1926), no. 8; *Essays in Honour of William Gallacher* (1961), no. 64; *First Hymn to Lenin* (1931), nos 33, 34, 43; *In Memoriam James Joyce* (1950), no. 51; *A Kist of Whistles* (1947), no. 25; *Lucky Poet* (1943), nos 4, 7, 24, 26, 31, 38, 49, 52, 55, 60; *The Modern Scot* (1931), no. 2; *Penny Wheep* (1926), no. 41; *Poems to Paintings by William Johnstone 1933* (1963), nos 20, 21; *Poetry Scotland No. 1* (1943), no. 53; *Poetry Scotland No. 4* (1949), nos 54, 63; *Sangschaw* (1925), nos 1, 3; *Sangs o' the Stane* (1951), no. 58; the *Scotsman* newspaper, nos 29, 67; *Second Hymn to Lenin* (1935), nos 9, 12, 13, 14, 18, 30, 35, 42, 44, 45, 46, 47, 48, 66; *Speaking for Scotland* (1946), no. 27; *Stony Limits* (1934), nos 11, 23, 32, 39, 65; *Voice of Scotland* Vol. II (1946), no. 15; Vol. III (1947), no. 59; Vol. IV (1947), no. 16; Vol. VI (1955), nos 19, 36; Vol. IX (1958), no. 50.

CONTENTS

FOREWORD

Christopher Murray Grieve was born on 11 August 1892, in the small town of Langholm, Dumfriesshire. His mother's family was of agricultural stock and his father came from a family of mill-workers. So right from the beginning he entered into a working-class inheritance, into 'the flower and iron of the truth'. His Scottish inheritance was just as closely defined, for Langholm is only a few miles from the English border and he was very conscious from childhood of being Scottish and not English: 'Above all, there was the frontier spirit — the sense of difference from, and not infrequently hatred of, the English which I certainly inherited to the full, and which later developed into my lifework' (*Lucky Poet*, p.16).

From childhood, too, he was conscious and proud of his class origins, and helped by the rich, vigorous and varied language of the Scottish borders, his sense of nationality and class became closely identified: 'This class antagonism has been strong in me from the very start: when I was a boy to speak English was to "speak fine", and the very thought of anything of the sort was intolerable' (*Lucky Poet*, p.17). It is remarkable that 80 years on, not only in the Borders but all over Scotland, in city, town and countryside, there are still hundreds of thousands of working-class children (and adults) who retain these sentiments and use, often aggressively, some form of the Scots language to assert their class awareness — and this despite a continuing process of acculturation by the education system and the media.

But the young Grieve inherited further gifts which were to stand him in good stead in his life's work as a poet:

> Border life was raw, vigorous, rich, bawdy and simply bursting with life and gusto. And the true test of my own work — since that is what I have sought to do — is the measure in which it has recaptured something of that unquenchable humour, biting satire, profound wisdom

> cloaked in bantering gaiety and the wealth of mad humour, with not a trace of whimsy, in the general leaping, light-hearted, reckless assault upon all conventions of dull respectability. (*Lucky Poet*, p.6).

And the Borders had other gifts to bestow. It was the home of the great ballads (*vide* Walter Scott's *Minstrelsy of the Scottish Borders*) and for a keen young mind this was a fine inspiration and a happy inheritance, giving an early familiarity with some of the finest poetry of the Scottish past.

And here, too, was the historic home of the reivers, the Scottish freebooters, who with their constant raids into England had kept up the 'frontier spirit' and acted as front-line fighters against English ascendancy over Scotland; a wild, reckless, highly individualist, band of fighting men who were determined to make their own law and assert their independence against all comers.

These two influences were to leave a marked impression on the future poet. As he says himself:

> Reivers to weavers and to me, Weird way!
> Yet in the last analysis I've sprung
> Frae battles mair than ballads, and it seems
> The thrawn auld watter has at last upswung
> Through me, and's mountin' like the vera devil
> To it's richt level.

But perhaps the greatest gift he received from his homeland was open access to the wide world of books. His father was a rural postman and the family lived in the post-office buildings. The Langholm library, the nucleus of which had been left by Thomas Telford, the famous engineer, was upstairs: 'I had constant access to it and used to fill a big washing-basket with books and bring it downstairs as often as I wanted to . . . . There were upwards of 12,000 books in the library . . . and I could go up in the dark and find any book I wanted' (*Lucky Poet*, p.8).

And so began his enormous appetite for reading everything, which was to develop into a life-long habit. He absorbed the thoughts and inspirations of the greatest writers of the past: poetry, philosophy, theology, politics, linguistics, the sciences, history, aesthetics, literature of all kinds and the cultures of four continents, his encyclopaedic mind noting and retaining the essentials which he required for his own writing. He became equally *au fait* with all the modern and advanced thinking and writing of his own day and his mind developed into a veritable store-house of world thought, which he could tap at any time as his habit of multiple reference and quotation clearly indicates.

In Marxist terms he was completely familiar with the 'plurality of superstructures' and was to be engaged all his life in unremitting attack on false doctrines and false consciouness, trying to bend every element of human thought to his own creative, strategic purposes, and at the same time to use every positive element within the superstructures, as they existed, as weapons against the economic determinism of Capitalist society — a massive operation in dialectics with one great end in mind:

> In establishing a right good fellowship
> Forever free of the belly-grip.

He had been active in the Socialist movement since his mid-teens and was to continue to be so from then on as a journalist, public speaker, literary critic and propagandist at all levels, but it was after his demobilisation in 1920 that he began to emphasise more strongly the Home Rule aspect which had always been an integral part of Scottish socialism. And in the early 1920s he began a full-scale battle for political and cultural independence for Scotland. In his *Contemporary Scottish Studies* he carried out a radical revaluation of modern Scottish literature and culture generally — a fundamental clearing of the ground in a series of essays which swept away much of the detritus which had gathered since the time of Burns, essays which were remarkable for the accuracy of his prophecies as to which talents would emerge as the important ones.

At the same time he was engaged in a series of political controversies with the one aim in mind: to counter all the false thinking which set Scottish Nationalism against Socialist Internationalism to the detriment of both Scotland and Socialism.

It was remarkable, then, in the midst of all this political and cultural turmoil, charge and counter-charge, denunciation and polemic, that the arch-agitator and originator of all the uproar should burst forth as a great new lyric poet. *Sangschaw* came out in 1925 and *Penny Wheep* in 1926, and those who knew what poetry was about (there were very few according to MacDiarmid) realised that a great turning-point had been reached in Scottish poetry. The lyrics in these two collections were startlingly new, and different in language, style and content from anything that had preceded them. MacDiarmid had mastered the Scots language and was releasing from it qualities of utterance that no one had suspected the existence of: rich and fantastic in texture and imagery, they were at the same time clean, clear and stark in their highly imaginative expression; realistic yet mysterious, cosmic yet earthy, particular and universal at one and the same time — a remarkable example of dialectical skill and poetic mastery.

Had MacDiarmid been interested only in making a reputation for himself as a poet, he could have continued to turn out these amazing lyrics and quickly established his name and fame in Scottish (and European) literature as a great lyric poet. But as Alexander Scott says in his foreword to the *Hugh MacDiarmid Anthology:* 'No Scottish poet had ever had a finer command of the lyric cry; and none has been less content with it'.

MacDiarmid, the restless, intransigent, Cameronian extremist, was not to be wiled away from his major objective of a resurgent Scotland, by promises of 'ease in Zion':

> A Scottish poet maun assume
> The burden o his people's doom
> And dee to brak' their livin' tomb.

He had no intention of resting on his laurels or anywhere else:

> My grave's no bad; they've put intill't
> Twa o' the Sassenachs I killt.
> I'll kill them again as sune as the horn
> Toots on the Resurrection Morn.

And so in 1926, the same year as *Penny Wheep*, he published a long dramatic poem, or poem-sequence, under the title *A Drunk Man Looks at the Thistle*. The struggle for the soul of Scotland had really begun, with the poet as the Drunk Man and the Thistle as the national emblem, which undergoes constant transmogrification and assumes many ugsome guises and distorted forms to hide its failure to flower as a true emblem of Scottish nationhood. In other words, it is a denunciation of all the evasions, side-steppings, back-slidings, treacheries, cowardice and failures of the Scots to break out from their 'living tomb' and take up their historic mission as a proud and independent nation, free to release their hidden riches and bestow them bountifully on the world at large, free to help take mankind one step higher in the scale of Civilisation.

Like many other detachable sections of the *Drunk Man*, the 'Ballad of the General Strike' is a complete poem in itself. Occurring halfway through the longer poem, it is central to the whole work, for it is here that MacDiarmid catches sight of the Thistle as it could and should be, the noble, heroic emblem of the embattled working class engaged in major confrontation with Capitalism. The contrary shapes, the ugsome guises, the feckless growth, the shank and jags of the perverse plant are changed utterly and even the royal purple is subsumed into a blazing, republican red, as the pin-head flowers and 'scrunts o' bloom' burgeon gloriously and burst into

> A reid, reid rose that in the lift
> Like a ball o' fire burned.

And for MacDiarmid this is the true flower of Scotland (peace be to his 'Little White Rose' of Scottish Nationalism, which has drawn far too much attention — and contention — from the critics).

But only too quickly the moment of glory burns itself out. The 'reid, reid rose' of promise disintegrates as suddenly as it had blossomed, as betrayal, lack of nerve and cowardice reassert their 'ancient vicious sway'. All that is left of the true Thistle is the embers and the ashes — and the bitter taste on the tongue of the poet as he watches the Devils dancing round exulting in their victory.

For the working class the collapse of the General Strike was a major defeat, which lead to further defections and betrayals and to long, long years of demoralisation. But for MacDiarmid, the poet, there was no defeat and no demoralisation for in the *Drunk Man* he had achieved a major poetic success. He had taken in all the wonder and magic of his earlier lyrics and gone beyond them, and had extended the scope of his imagination and the wealth and use of his language in a powerful, original way. He was now completely battle-hardened and more determined than ever to carry on the fight. He was soon back in print, in 1927, with *Albyn, or Scotland and the Future*, in which he made a complete re-assessment of the state of Scotland, politically and culturally. At the same time he was engaged in furious political activity (in company with Cunninghame Graham,

Compton MacKenzie, Erskine of Mar and other prominent personalities) which led to the founding in 1928 of the National Party of Scotland — from which party, incidentally, he was to be expelled four years later (after a take-over by the moderates) for Communist deviation from the Nationalist line.

But in addition to those other activities MacDiarmid had been developing his preparations for a new major attack in the poetry field. Strongly influenced by Erskine of Mar's ideas on Celtic Communism (just as John MacLean had been in the early 1920s), and further inspired by his reading of the great Irish poets of the past, he was determined to bring all the resources of the Gaelic Idea into his fight against English imperialist ascendancy:

Scots steel tempered wi' Irish fire
Is the weapon that I desire.

It may have been his intention to make a direct frontal attack as he had done in the *Drunk Man*, but in the event what did emerge was a guerilla campaign of considerable importance:

O the lion is aff the flag again
And reengin' the countryside.

The new National Party had failed to make any impact and the working class, with MacDonaldism rampant, was in a state of hopeless confusion, but MacDiarmid was not confused: the fight would go on:

O the lion is oot o' the flag again
And whiles I feel't in ma hert
— Ramsay Macdonald claimed to be Scots
And I crunched him for a stert.

MacDiarmid's long poem, *To Circumjack Cencrastus*, subtitled *The Curly Snake*, came out in 1930 and was twice as long as the *Drunk Man*. Into this volume he threw everything available. He had referred to the *Drunk Man* before its publication as a 'gallimaufry', i.e. a lucky-bag of bits and pieces, but in its final form the poem had turned out to have a convincing original architecture of its own. And so, too, with *Cencrastus* where the architecture was inspirational, a kind of organised lawlessness, which made the poem much more of a 'guerillamaufry' than a gallimaufry. And that is how we should see it, for MacDiarmid, the reiver chief, is engaged on a series of spoiling attacks on both sides of the border against the English overlords and their Scottish lackeys and he has called in the Highland caterans and the 'wild Irishry' as reinforcements: the MacDonalds, the MacLeods, the MacCodrums, the Raffertys, O'Reillys and O'Sullivans, all as spirited and battle-hardened as himself. The common emblem is not the Thistle but the Curly Snake, which represents not only all the sinuosities of ancient Celtic wisdom but also the devious resourcefulness of MacDiarmid himself, who has said of the winding path near Langholm called the Curly Snake: 'It has always haunted my imagination and has probably constituted itself the ground-plan and pattern of my mind'. The Borderers, the Highlanders and the Irish were going to hold the line against English imperialism by using guerilla tactics, darting and thrusting, coiling and uncoiling, in and out through the enemy — until the time came for a major offensive . . . .

But would the time ever come? MacDiarmid shows very clearly in 'Lourd on ma Hert' that he is well aware of the cursed time-lag (in both the short term and the long term) that lies between Scotland and her destiny. Wry, dry, laconic, ironic, the poem achieves a beautiful dialectical balance between the optimism of the will and the pessimism (realism, fatalism) of the intellect.

In 'Unconscious Goal of History' there is the same balance of will and intellect, but the irony and humour have been dropped in favour of a deep, passionate interest in the outcome and an utter determination to use any weapon he can to influence it:

Sae that my people frae their living graves
May loup and play a part in History yet.

The short poem 'Separatism' states quite explicitly what the leap should be: to complete, independent nationhood. But the part that Scotland has to play in history is even more important and the 'Golden Lyric' (*Collected Poems*) shows symbolically what that role is: to fight against Capitalism, Philistinism and everything which is inimical to the full flowering of the spirit of mankind

For this in the last resort
Mak's them less apes mair men
And leads their leaders albeit
They're owre blin' to see it.

And in 'To Hell wi' Happiness' his determination is expressed in terms of total, savage intransigence. There can be no compromise, no alternative:

> 'The beaten track is *beaten* frae the stert'.

And so the will and the intellect must be united in one superordinate compulsion:

> I sing the terrifying discipline
> O' the free mind that gars a man
> Mak' his joys kill his joys.
> The weakest by the strongest
> The temporal by the fundamental
> (Or hope o' the fundamental)

This is MacDiarmid, the extremist, at his Cameronian best. If Cencrastus was not to be circumjacked, then neither was MacDiarmid.

In the 1930s MacDiarmid was caught up in a maelstrom of events which would have shattered the confidence of the vast majority of men. His health undermined, with no possibility of employment, with his marriage and family life completely broken up, he was at the receiving end of all the buffets that fortune had to offer, but through sheer indomitability of will he rose above them and not only continued the fight but extended it and developed it. It was in fact the most fully fertile period of his whole career as a poet. He was in abject poverty and had to withdraw to the remote island of Whalsay in the Shetlands with his second wife, Valda Trevlyn, whose constant resourcefulness and inspired practicality in matters of food, fuel, furniture and shelter kept them just barely above subsistence level for a long period of years (*vide* Michael Grieve's introduction to the *Hugh MacDiarmid Anthology*).

But despite all this MacDiarmid maintained his position at the centre of affairs as agitator-in-chief. *Scots Unbound*, *Stony Limits*, *Scottish Scene* (with Lewis Grassic Gibbon), *Scottish Eccentrics*, *Lucky Poet* and the Hymns to Lenin and much more in prose and verse came pouring from his pen during these years as he kept up the fight for Scotland, Gaeldom, Socialism and the whole long-term future of mankind.

MacDiarmid, of course, was already a Marxist, albeit a very idiosyncratic one, who was determined not to concede a single point to any stereotype thinking that Communism might produce. He joined the Communist Party in 1934 and was expelled in 1937 for Nationalist deviation, reinstated on appeal, then expelled again in 1938. But this to-and-fro of Party membership made no difference to his Marxism. What did make a difference was the objective political and economic situation: unemployment, Fascism, Civil War in Spain and the inability of Nationalism and Socialism to make any real headway against increasingly aggressive Imperialism.

He was drawn more and more to Leninism. He admired Lenin's obduracy of will, his no-nonsense approach to the establishment of the Workers' State, his emphasis on organisation, his complete identification with the working class, his masterly sense of timing and his all-embracing grasp of dialectics.

In the *First Hymn* he sees Lenin as marking the greatest turning-point in history since Christ and a more important one since his work opens up richer possibilities for the advance of mankind, Lenin's secret lies

> No' in the majority will that accepts the result
> But in the real will that bides its time and kens
> The benmaist resolve is the poo'er.

In the *Second Hymn* MacDiarmid grants that Lenin is the 'saviour of Civilisation', much more than the great poets because of his organic constructional work and practicality:

> Naething is dune save as we ha'e
> Means to en's transparently fitted.

But he goes on to point out that if poetry can 'cut the cackle and pursue real ends', if the poet can acquire the power of Lenin's vision, if he can make his knowledge as exact and complete as Lenin's,

> Unremitting, relentless
> Organised to the last degree,

then poetry will become the core of all activity. And he concludes:

> Ah, Lenin, politics is bairn's play
> To what this maun be.

This may sound patronising on MacDiarmid's part but this is in no way the case. MacDiarmid has complete respect for Lenin's work in freeing a large section of humanity from the tyranny of 'breid an' butter politics', but the ending of the 'belly-grip' is only the beginning of the real history of mankind — 'freein' oor poo'ers for greater things'.

Lenin could be caustic, scathing, bitingly sardonic and denunciatory — just like MacDiarmid — with his fellow revolutionaries, but with the ordinary worker he used a different approach, patiently explaining, linking his propaganda to the direct experience of the worker, talking to him seriously at his present level of consciousness, not at some arbitrary point. And in the 'Seamless Garment' MacDiarmid does the very same, a model example of Leninism in practice. This gives the poem a fundamental richness of style and content, into which the natural conversational rhythm, the popular language and idiom and the imagery drawn from every-day, working-class experience are beautifully interwoven, so that the very richness of the weave brings out the message 'clean, clear and exact':

> There's a play o' licht frae the factory windas
> Could ye no' mak mair yoursel?

Years later MacDiarmid's commitment to Leninism was even greater when he wrote the 'Third Hymn'. Glasgow was still a stickit Petrograd and the memory of the 'Red Clyde' was buried under betrayals, lies and false gospel. MacDiarmid can do nothing with Glasgow and calls for Lenin's help:

> You turned a whole world right side up
> With no dramatic gesture, no memorable word
> *Now measure Glasgow for a like laconic overthrow.*

Glasgow is a city of the abyss:

> A horror that might sicken your stomach even
> The peak of the capitalist system and the trough of Hell.

MacDiarmid goes on to give an appalling picture of the misery of the people, their poverty and their mindlessness and the complete absence of hope — and the evil forces threatening them:

> . . . the gangsters lurk, the officer class, ruthless,
> Watching Glasgow's every step and lusting to attack her.

But the will to resist has gone and the people are deaf and blind to their danger:

> And most insidious and stultifying of all
> The anti-human forces have instilled the thought
> That knowledge has outrun the human brain

> . . .and so have turned
> Humanity's vast achievements against the human mind.

And here MacDiarmid conveys a tremendous sense of outrage, for his most fundamental beliefs are being attacked, and he thunders out his denunciation:

> This is the lie of lies—the High Treason to Mankind.

Only some great illumination can light up this City of Darkness. The scientists and poets are spent forces, lost in the side-alleys and dead-ends of compromise and betrayal, and MacDiarmid turns to Lenin, the 'Fire of Freedom', to make his final appeal:

> Spirit of Lenin, light on this city now!
> Light up this city now!

The 'Third Hymn' is a remarkable poem with high tension running right through it. The constant movement of changing tone, argument and setting, the heightened realism of the various 'shots' give it the best qualities of dramatic documentary, and at the same time the many disparate elements (including the prose blocks from Bolitho and Carlile) integrate directly into the movement by shock and excitement overcoming the need for any ordinary linkage. Added to these effects, sustaining them and vibrating through them, is the constant interplay of MacDiarmid's insistent, urgent demand for a solution and the vivid, dynamic working of Lenin's 'great constructive, synthesising mind'. This is a powerful modern poem — even overpowering — and is certainly political poetry of a very high order.

Just as MacDiarmid had been more and more attracted to Lenin and Leninism by the pressure of events so also was he attracted to the ideas of the great Scottish Leninist, John MacLean. MacLean, who was the most outstanding revolutionary that Britain has ever produced, had been the architect of the 'Red Clyde', the great proletarian upsurge in Scotland during and immediately after the First World War. He had led the tremendous fight against the war and the 'Hands off Russia' and 'Hands off Ireland' campaigns. He was elected an Honorary President of the First All-Russian Congress of Soviets with Lenin, Trotsky, Liebknecht and Adler; and Lenin himself had appointed him as Bolshevik Consul in Glasgow in 1918. Three times jailed for sedition by the British Government, who recognised him as the most 'dangerous' man they had to deal with because of his extensive teaching of Marxism all over Scotland and because of his enormous agitational influence on the Scottish working class, he stood out as an epic figure even in his own day. But as well as being the most extreme Socialist of his time he became the most extreme Nationalist as well and an out-and-out champion of Gaeldom.

Influenced by Lenin, James Connolly and Erskine of Mar and by events in Ireland, in India, in Europe and at home, and increasingly disenchanted with the London leadership of British Socialism, he struck out for a break-away, separatist Scottish Workers' Republic. It was this combination of extreme Socialism and extreme Nationalism that appealed to MacDiarmid, and even more so the character of the man himself: the man of indomitable will, the man who did not recognise the word 'retreat', the man who was prepared to sacrifice everything — his job, his family, his health, his life — in the interests of his class because, as Nan Milton writes in *John MacLean*, the biography of her father, 'his class, its sorrows, its struggles, had become his life and being'.

It is easy to see how a man like John MacLean could influence MacDiarmid and permanently capture his imagination. And that is exactly what happened, for MacDiarmid broke completely with the official Nationalists and for the next four decades constantly put forward his Red Scotland thesis — his short-hand form of it: 'Scottish Workers' Republicanism à la John MacLean' became a permanent slogan — as the only true line for the advance of Socialism in the British Isles. MacLean's ideas and message had been buried under a slag-hill of lies and betrayals, under constitutionalism, accommodationism and plain downright charlatanism, and it is to MacDiarmid's eternal credit that he fought so long and so persistently to 'countermand the betrayal' of MacLean. And he has succeeded, for nowadays there is not one leading activist in the Scottish movement — Socialist or Nationalist — who does not understand in some degree the importance of MacLean's work and the permanent central position he holds in Scottish politics.

His two poems on MacLean, therefore, have a special significance. Nowhere else is MacDiarmid so splendidly, savagely subversive as in the longer poem, 'John MacLean'. This is the Class War. This is the Red Republic. This is the poem his publishers were afraid to publish. All MacDiarmid's pent-up hatred of Capitalism and of its power to thwart and stultify the noblest aspirations of mankind is released into a seething torrent of prophetic denunciation, for John MacLean had been the one true chance of Scotland fulfilling her destiny, the one 'flash of sun in a country all prison-grey' and he had been viciously undone by the British establishment and all its

> . . . ministers and lawyers,
> Hulking brutes of police, fat bourgeoisie,
> Sleek derma for congested guts . . . .

and MacDiarmid is out for blood and retribution:

> Speak to others of Christian charity; I cry again
> For vengeance on the murderers of John MacLean.

When MacDiarmid reads this poem to a Scottish working-class audience, as he has frequently done in recent years, there is a hush of wonderment. Half the wonder is for the greatness of MacLean, the other half is sheer admiration for the intense, blood-and-guts, total commitment of MacDiarmid to MacLean's memory and message.

The shorter poem, 'Krassivy', is equally compelling but works in an entirely different way. It starts with a quiet, calm, authoritative statement, which immediately commands our attention and excitement because it is so all-embracing and breath-taking in its sweep. Then it moves on, not by way of argument but by comparison and revelation, so that we are completely caught up in the wonder of the message. This is conveyed by a beautifully cadenced phrasing which, though natural and even conversational, contains a hypnotic quality of rising excitement as the poem moves with a sense of step-by-step inevitability to identify the greatness of Lenin with the greatness of MacLean. The incantatory use and repetition of the magic word 'krassivy' is the culminating master-stroke which leads to the final, unchallengeable statement of MacLean's uniqueness and at the same time carries us right back through the poem and its every detail to the quiet calm of the opening statement. And so the whole poem has a rich glowing unity of human warmth — Russian and Scottish and universal.

The late Sydney Goodsir Smith, the greatest Scottish poet after MacDiarmid, was also a highly committed Scottish Republican and wrote some powerful poetry on MacLean. In his famous 'Ballant o' John MacLean' there are two lines which sum up succinctly the essential message and contrast of MacDiarmid's two poems:

He won the hate o' the monger breed
But the love o' his ain was strang.

MacLean had been a legend in his own day and the poets of Scotland, following MacDiarmid, strengthened it, confirmed it and made it permanent. As Nan Milton writes in *John MacLean:* 'Thus as a result of the Scottish literary renaissance, which he himself had helped to inspire, the legend took on a new immortal form'.

MacDiarmid is often considered to be a 'difficult' poet and it is true that certain obscurities do occur in his poetry because he is dealing with very complex matters or because we are ignorant of his references or unfamiliar with the totality of his thinking. But there is a complete absence of obscurantism in his work. Once we have a general idea of the nature of his Nationalism, Socialism and Republicanism and of his tremendous concern for the full release of the spirituality of man, we find the bulk of the poems in this collection clear, direct and explicit propaganda for Socialism. As he says himself in 'Poetry and Propaganda':

In short any utterance that is not pure
Propaganda is impure propaganda for sure.

His poems on Spain or against tyranny and Fascism are splendid examples of this pure propaganda and a poem like the 'Belly-Grip' just asks to be read aloud to a mass audience. When a poet like Hamish Henderson does so the effect is gripping indeed: the audience rises to the poem in fresh, clear awareness of what Socialism really means. It is much more telling than a hundred political speeches. This is the power of MacDiarmid's propaganda — fresh, clear and exciting.

In his poems against religious superstition the message is equally clear, whether expressed directly as in 'After 2,000 Years', with a snort of contempt as in the Billy Graham poem or, as in 'Plaster Madonna', by an explicit underlining of the serious danger of spurious miracles and false gospel. And the message is the same as Richard Carlile's:

Superstition will not treat or covenant. They must be
uprooted
Completely for public and individual safety.

When dealing with the weaknesses of the working class, he

is just as ruthlessly direct. 'Joy in the 20th Century' is a scathing mockery of economism, and in the poem 'In the Gangs' (which is an extract from a long Glasgow poem on the lumpenism of large sections of the proletariat), he shows clearly and clinically the nature of the dangerous mindlessness which arises from false consciousness. And his criticism of such decadent thinking is expressed with quite savage directness in poems like 'At the Cenotaph', 'Reflections in an Ironworks' and 'Think not that I Forget', where MacDiarmid from the aristocratic height of full Socialist consciousness denounces the awful, corrupting unawareness which keeps the workers in servitude to Capitalism.

In his poems on royalty he is still concerned with the foolish blindness of the people, with their failure to reject the parasitism, hypocrisy and fraud inherent in all royal occasions. This is brought out vigorously in 'Royal Wedding Gifts' and in 'In the Children's Hospital', and with splendid satirical simplicity in 'Die Grenzsituation':

> When — while the whole world held its silly breath —
> She gave it her own holy name — as sure as death!. . .
> And not one honest soul in Glasgow, or Christendom, laughed!
> It seemed — and was — as though she'd stricken all mankind daft.

Turning to his other poems of occasion we find MacDiarmid using the same direct clarity to convey his message. He had rejoined the Communist Party in 1957 and had become more and more friendly with Willie Gallacher, the Party chairman and its most beloved and outstanding member. 'A Sprig of White Heather', written in honour of Gallacher's eightieth birthday, is an unstinted, warm-hearted salute from one veteran Socialist to another. It leaps into life and lifts straight off the page with detail upon detail to show the character and essential greatness of the man:

> Willie Gallacher shines out, single of purpose
> Lovely in his integrity, exemplifying
> All that is best in public service — distinct,
> Clear-headed and clean-hearted,
> A great humanist, true comrade and friend.

Daniel Cohn-Bendit, the leader of the great student uprising in France, is equally highly honoured by MacDiarmid but in a much more impersonal way. In his poem 'For Daniel Cohn-Bendit' there are no character details, no personal references, not even his name is mentioned. The poem is simply a detailed, spelled-out explicit statement on any man's right to resist unjust government:

> No man or group of men has any right
> To force another man or other groups of men
> To do anything he or they do not wish to do.
> There is no right to govern without
> The consent of the governed.

This is what 1968 was all about. This was Cohn-Bendit's credo and MacDiarmid endorses it completely.

The remaining poem of occasion, 'On the Asportation of the Scone Stone', marks a very important occasion indeed, for the retrieval of the Stone of Destiny from Westminster Abbey on Christmas Day 1950 was the greatest turning-point in Scotland's destiny since the time of the Red Clyde. The holy sanctuary of British Imperialism had been breached and the sacred totem was gone. The Scottish people matured overnight and England was now on the defensive. This was the real beginning of the rise of Nationalism and the break-up of the United Kingdom:

> A little nation marks the opening
> Of a like unequal battle for its own
> And splits the atom of Earth's greatest throne.

The retrieval of the Stone appealed to everything in MacDiarmid: to the Border Reiver, to the Nationalist, to the Socialist, to the Republican and to the Poet with all his belief in the power of symbols. But it is as the Prophet that he declares himself, emphasising and italicising the inevitability of what is going to happen:

> *Far more, O England, than the Scone Stone's gone,*
> *And all the King's horses and the King's men*
> *Cannot set up your Humpty Dumpty again.*

Thirty years later we can all see how truly prophetic this poem was.

Behind the prophecy, of course, and inspiring it, is MacDiarmid's clear understanding of the importance of symbols. David and Goliath, the Stone of Destiny, the King's horses and men and Humpty Dumpty are all strong symbols in themselves and particularly felicitous in conjunction with the symbolic nature of the event they commemorate, for MacDiarmid, while not a Symbolist in the classic French sense, is a poet of symbols *par excellence*. In 'Behind the Symbols', referring to the eagle and the red stag, he gives his rationale:

> For these are among Earth's glorious symbols
> To souls of men needing symbols yet
> And a man must be well-nourished on these
> To embrace the Infinite.

His use of the symbol is varied. Sometimes he just presents the symbol and leaves it to do its own work, sometimes as in the 'Skeleton of the Future' he gives it a minimal development to suggest its full significance, and sometimes the symbolism only emerges at the end of the poem. In 'Hostings of Heroes', for example, where in the last line we suddenly see the 'crawl of cockroaches' in total contrast with the magnificence of Gaeldom's ancient heroic grandeur, we realise that the whole poem is a symbol of the decline and fall of Scotland through the ages. Similarly in 'Golden Wine in the Gaidhealtachd' (*Collected Poems*), although the symbol — whisky — is mentioned right from the first line, it is only in the last three lines that we begin to catch the full symbolical significance of the poem:

> Symbolising the holy virtues of hospitality and social kindness.
> Through what else can Scotland recover its poise
> Save, as Very Hope believes, this golden wine yet?

And as we go back over the poem we realise that it is not just a poem about whisky, or hospitality, or Scotland, but is primarily a poem of universal human brotherhood built on the recognition and acceptance of the rich, peculiar differences of nations, of regions, of even the smallest community.

The same universal human brotherhood is brought out in 'With the Herring Fishers' by an entirely different use of the symbol. The poem starts off as a pure documentary of the fisherman at work. The language is the rich, racy language of the fishermen themselves, a language of work experience, of traditional community endeavour, of exclusive Shetland identity:

'Soom on, bonnie herring, soom on', they shout,
Or 'Come in, O come in, and see me'.
'Come gie the auld man something to dae.
It'll be a braw change frae the sea'.

Then suddenly this rich, particular, exclusive identity of social effort is transformed half-way through the poem into an all-embracing, universal oneness of human effort and we find God (a symbol for the universal) speaking in the same rich Shetland work language not to the herring but to all mankind:

'Left, right — O come in and see me',
Reid and yellow and black and white
Toddlin' up into Heaven thegither
At peep o' day frae the endless night.

The Shetland fishermen have become, through the very particularity of their work identity, the symbol of working men everywhere.

But MacDiarmid is not only a master of the symbol, he is equally master of the short dramatic presentation, and when he combines the two, as in 'Old Wife in High Spirits' we get a particularly happy effect. The transformation of the old woman from 'a mere rickle o' banes' into the 'heich skeich auld cat' is vivid and immensely human in itself, but when we see her as the representative of her class and as a symbol of the rich potential of that class to transcend its own limitations — and, in so doing, to transform the whole of society — the poem takes on an extra exciting dimension of life which the bourgeoisie can never share for, as MacDiarmid concludes:

Ninety per cent o' respectable folk never hae
As muckle life in their creeshy carcases
As kythed in that wild auld carline that day!

The same combination of the dramatic and the symbolic helps to make 'Kandym in the Waste Land' one of MacDiarmid's greatest poems, for the intensely dramatic, dialectical struggle of the kandym to maintain itself against the desert sands is multi-symbolic: will against circumstance, growth against sterility, civilisation against barbarism, the vital against the void; in short, the totally uncompromising spirit of MacDiarmid himself:

My songs are kandym in the Waste Land.

But this dramatic operation of the symbol occurs again and again, always in a different manner but always with the same effect of bringing out the message with an exciting, vivid clarity. In 'The Bonnie Broukit Bairn' where MacDiarmid first declares his commitment to *Diesseitigkeit*, Earth, the symbol of humanity and all its travails, is glorified and vivified beyond its rivals with such a lovely, living tenderness that all the varied beauty of the heavens pale into nullity. And in poems like 'Crowdieknowe' and 'The Second Flood' the symbols operate with such a strong folk momentum that we find it easy to identify with the muckle men of Langholm — symbolising, even in their graves, the rich roaring life of the Borders — and, paradoxically, with the Gairds o' Heaven sweeping away all the douce, kirk-going bourgeoisie of Langholm — and everywhere else.

In 'The Storm-Cock's Song', despite the stark, bare setting and the cold, bleak absence of all promise, the poem lifts and keeps lifting in bold, triumphant song exalting the power of will and spirit:

> His 'Will I do it? Do it I will!' is worth a lot
> When the rest have nothing at all to say.

And in 'Glasgow 1960' we have perhaps the most unusual symbol of all: the symbol of the fictional abstruse to represent the importance of the real abstruse. This ought to produce a really difficult poem but because of the dead-pan, anecdotal, spoof technique, which especially appeals to the sophisticated Glasgow sense of humour, the message comes out as clear as any other. As one Glasgow shop steward summed it up: 'It's quite clear what MacDiarmid's saying: he's saying it's like what it's no' like the day, but it's no' gonna be like what it's no' like the morra'. Could any academic sum it up better?

In a long, 50,000 words essay on 'Aesthetics in Scotland' — still unpublished — MacDiarmid states:

> I regard the cultural question of supreme importance, and believe the function of Literature and the Arts to be the expansion of human consciousness, or as my friend Sean O'Casey termed it, 'the sensitive extension of the world'. So in my own writing I am not concerned

> to purvey 'what the people want', or to cater for any 'ready-made public'. This is why I have said, amongst other things, 'As a Socialist I am interested only in a very subordinate way in the politics of Socialism as a political theory; my real concern with Socialism is as an artist's organised approach to the interdependencies of life'.

This statement may come as a surprise from a man who is known all over the world as a great political poet. And as we have seen, his political poetry is in no way subordinate to any of his other poetry. It may be regarded as one special aspect of his poetic vision, but it certainly cannot be discounted as being of mere tangential importance. What MacDiarmid is emphasising in this statement, in fact, is that socialist politics is only one part of the sum total of human experience. He is concerned with strategy much more than tactics, with long-term ends much more than short-term means, with the end-product of human potential much more than any immediate political gain; and above all he is much less concerned with politics, 'the art of the possible', than with poetry, the art of transcending the possible, and the most highly sensitive instrument of spirit, psyche and mind.

In some of his shorter poems we have the feeling that they are emanating from an atmosphere of brooding ratiocination, from a keen probing mind intensely occupied with producing sharper and sharper insights to extend the vision of human experience.

In 'A Point in Time', one of the 'Poems to Paintings by William Johnstone', MacDiarmid achieves the impossible by presenting us with a *still-life* conception of the immensely dynamic idea of 'the interdependencies of life' — and all in nine lines, in one single concentrated flash of illumination. In 'Conception', another poem from the same collection, we are taken right into the heart of MacDiarmid's brooding self-examination:

> Something growing up, within my own
> Separated and isolated lonely being,
> Within the deep dark of my own consciousness

and we share in the 'strange, mysterious, awful finding' that Scotland is not external to him but growing up *inside* his consciousness like a foetus in the womb, so that he is carrying the very life of his people within his own and this gives his Nationalism, his love for Scotland, a very special identity:

> Not the Will to Power but the Will to Flower!

This is indeed a great conception in both senses of the word.

An equally intense shiver of awareness runs through us when we grasp the significance of the four-line poem 'On the Ocean Floor'. Here MacDiarmid, preoccupied with genius working at a peak point of recognition, suddenly sets against it the tens of thousand of anonymous generations who have sunk into the darkness of oblivion — of history and pre-history — like the tiny chalky shells of the dying foraminifera sinking slowly to the ocean bed. And he communicates to us his own sharp awareness of the innumerable dead just as Dante does in the *Inferno*:

> I had not thought, they were so numberless,
> That Death such countless legions had undone.

It is worthy of note that these two lines of Dante have often been mentioned by MacDiarmid as the two best lines of poetry ever written. With all respect to Edwin Morgan, there is no question in this poem of MacDiarmid forgetting the masses. Quite the contrary. He is humbly reminding himself of his obligation to make greater and greater efforts in the service of the living and in recognition of what he has inherited from the generations of the dead.

And it is with this same humility he approaches the question of poetic insight in another two short poems. In 'Light and Shadow' he is quite explicit on the need for constant vigilance so that no insight escapes:

> On every thought I have the countless shadows fall
> Of other thoughts as valid that I cannot have;
> Cross-lights of errors, too, impossible to me,
> Yet somehow truer than all those thoughts. . . .

Genius carries a tremendous responsibility and must always be tuned up to the highest pitch to receive the whole range of alternative insights which lie behind the immediate insights of the moment. And in a *cri de coeur* he adds:

> May I never lose these shadowy glimpses of unknown thoughts
> That modify and minify my own.

In 'O Ease my Spirit' the whole poem is a *cri de coeur* for

> . . . a more constant insight
> Into the fundamental similarity of all activities

so that the spiritual and the physical can be integrated into one single universality of experience, where it would be possible for the poet, totally at one with himself, to put out his hand to draw the whole round world to him in tender loving identity.

These short poems of insight, 'illuminations' of a very special kind, are as finely conceived and as cleanly executed as the famous early lyrics, but because of the intense dedication involved, the seriousness of purpose and the matureness of thought they must be considered as a great advance in MacDiarmid's poetry. Had he continued to produce poems of this kind he could have made another reputation for himself, as a poet of illuminations, as a poet's poet, as a poet of the creative process — but this was not his intention. He was as little content with these poems as he had been with the early lyrics except that they showed the way forward to what was to become his greatest and most important poetry.

As we have already noted MacDiarmid was very influenced by Lenin and, in particular, by his intellectuality:

> Not only an analytical mind but also
> A great constructive synthesizing mind
> Able to build up in thought the new reality
> As it must actually come.

This is exactly what MacDiarmid wanted to do for poetry and it is not surprising that he emphasises Lenin's insistence on the need for the synthesis of all human thought. In *Lucky Poet* he gives us the famous quotation from Lenin's last speech made to the Fourth Congress of the Communist International in November 1922 — as a matter of fact he gives us the quotation *twice*:

> Now for the first time we have the possibility of learning. I do not know how long this possibility will last. I do not know how long the capitalist powers will give us the opportunity of learning in peace and quietude. But we must utilize every moment in which we are free from war, that we may learn, and learn *from the bottom up* . . . . It would be a very serious mistake to suppose that one can become a Communist without

> making one's own the treasures of human knowledge. It would be mistaken to imagine that it is enough to adopt the Communist formulas and conclusions of Communist science, without mastering that sum-total of different branches of knowledge, the final outcome of which is Communism . . . . Communism becomes an empty phrase, a mere façade, and the Communist a mere bluffer, if he has not worked over in his consciousness the whole inheritance of human knowledge — made his own and worked over anew all that was of value in the more than two thousand years of development of human thought.

In his later work MacDiarmid takes Lenin quite literally. He was of course temperamentally three-quarters of the way there already, familiar with the 'plurality of superstructures', very much *au fait* with 'the sum-total of different branches of knowledge', but now, with enormous energy, he started to ransack every source of knowledge he could get at. In thousands and thousands of lines and in tens of thousands of quotations and references he built up a veritable treasure-house of poetry material. Poems gave way to longer and longer stretches of poetry in one huge epic effort to cover the totality of human knowledge. There have been many arguments about this later poetry of MacDiarmid but it is not our immediate concern to enter into such discussions except to say that if epic poetry has to be prepared in *advance* of the epic age of Communism there is no other way to do it. In 'Major Road Ahead' we can see what magnificent poetry MacDiarmid *can* write when he gets the chance of dealing with a living epic theme.

Our immediate concern in this volume of Socialist poems is not to deal with his later work at large but to make extracts from it which deal directly with Socialist poetry, in other words to give a brief idea of MacDiarmid's Marxist aesthetics, for it is in his poetry rather than in his prose that we get his sharpest definition of what Socialist poetry involves. In 'My Poetry is Marxist' he shows right away that it does *not* involve the churning out of a perpetuity of 'enchanting lyrics' when the needs of the day demand a totally different approach. Socialist poetry must be a poetry of today and not of the past, but it must have a great respect for the old heritage from which it stems and not deteriorate into 'a purely hothouse proletarian literature', which, in effect, reduces the stature of both the proletariat and of poetry itself.

And what are the needs of the day in poetry (art, literature)? In the poem 'Against Infantilism' MacDiarmid gets to the heart of the matter. Poetry must reflect

> The overcoming by life of its own limitations
> The calling out of the major images of the future,
> What and as is — and as should and will be
> Reality in motion, advancing and developing.

And how is the poet to do so? 'Against Infantilism' is addressed to the younger Scottish writers but, in effect, it applies to writers everywhere. The greatest need of the poet is to relate his art to the central issues of life. He must bring to his poetry:

> An immediate experience of the concrete,
> A rich overflowing apprehension of the definite
> Day-by-day content of our people's lives,
> A burningly clear understanding of the factors at work,
> Of the actual correlation of the forces, in labour to-day.

This is the centrality that gives value to his work. Any side-stepping, evasion or avoidance of this centrality is fatal. The poet must be

> Long past the affectation of being above the battle
> Of being socially agnostic, seeing all systems
> As subject to historic change, and the will
> Of great men, and accepting none.

He must eschew the temptation of fitting himself into any of the old 'schools' of poetry:

> Of realism, romanticism, classicism
> Naturalism, and all the witless rest
> Of isms, flourishing in the parent mire of scholasticism.
> The primary capitalistic neurosis is narcissism.

Capitalism has produced the fragmentation of man. He is increasingly alienated from his own labour, his society, his family and — most important — from himself. There is no oneness for him. He cannot be at one with his own experience, because he has no single centre to receive it, organise and integrate it, so that his actual, factual, social experience is continually falsified and transformed into false consciousness. He is more and more turned in on himself, farther and farther removed from the central issues of life. This neurosis may affect the poet in just the same way as anyone else, but it is his special duty to be more highly conscious of its workings and to combat it at every level. The poet's task is to integrate experience, not to become part of its disintegration.

MacDiarmid resolutely refuses any compromise with this neurosis of capitalism. There must be no capitulation to fragmentation, to alienation or to any kind of false consciousness. There must be no narcissism. The poet must not distort the content of life:

> In order to make it conform
> To some desperate personal wish-fulfilment
> Or flee from it entirely — into the past,
> Into fantasy, or some other reality-surrogate.

He must be aware that the so-called 'culture class' is no longer a repository of culture. As the crisis of capitalism develops the 'middle-class vanguard' reveals its moral weakness and intellectual poverty, and all that is left is a thin veneer of artistic sophistication. There is no 'culture class' left. And so the writer must become committed to the radical, revolutionary task of overthrowing capitalism:

> Man can find his own dignity only in action now.

And so, too, with the poet. The value of his writing

> Will be measured by the extent to which
> The dialectics of our era find expression
> In the artistic imagery — how widely, forcefully, clearly
> The burning contemporary problems are expressed in it,
> The class war, the struggles and ideals
> Of the proletariat bent on changing the world,
> And consequently on changing human nature.

In other words all infantilisms have been discredited, all options have been closed:

> Outside the revolutionary movement there is no place
> For any writer worth a moment's thought.

As an interesting side-light on this poem we find in the poem about Siegfried Sassoon, 'An English War-Poet', that MacDiarmid has scant regard for any 'culture class' at all. Apart from Sassoon's anti-war stand being so markedly contrasted with the real anti-war attitude of the International

Brigade, we see Sassoon himself as the representative — and victim — of that famous English institution the 'cult of the country gentleman', a cult which in its modified, genteel Scottish version did great damage to Burns by distracting him from his true audience, the common people of Ayrshire and Scotland. Through Sassoon and his attitudes MacDiarmid shows us the inherent weakness of all bourgeois culture classes, which are not built on culture but privilege, and which under pressure always fall back on privilege and accommodate their culture to it. Traditional values always win out over any attempted independence of mind. Patiently, gently, even benignly MacDiarmid takes Sassoon and his 'culture class' apart. Good food and golf, a clever psychiatrist and forty-five seconds of sympathy from members of the royal family restore him to sanity and he is as good as old, as muddled and as 'partially' dissatisfied with the universe as ever, 'with no real self-knowledge and no fixed scale of values'. He had rebelled under stress of feeling, then conformed again under stress of feeling, entirely the victim of his emotions. There is no evidence of a thinking mind, no psychological or philosophical substance, and so he 'falls back into the ranks', playing golf, chasing the fox, reading poetry. And MacDiarmid sums up the whole fallacy of 'culture class' with the pointed question:

> Is it too cynical to think at times
> That his real objection to the war
> Is its interfering with these pleasures?

Poetry can no longer be addressed to any 'culture class'. It can only be addressed to the people themselves. But to be effective it must stand for

> . . . production, use and life
> As opposed to property, profits and death.

In 'High, Low, Jack and the Goddamn Game' MacDiarmid shows how this can be done. The poet will be effective only if he can bring out clearly the disposition of class forces in society, showing how society

> Determines attitudes in its members
> By opening to them certain possibilities
> By induction into objectively recognised statuses
> While closing quite effectively other possibilities.

There must be no mysticism, no obscurantism, no

cendentalism, no organismic approach which ends up with some form of deity being the final arbiter of man's actions in society. In short the approach should be dialectical. But it must be thorough-going and rigorously scientific. MacDiarmid is always on guard against the quasi-dialectical which is selective of its material and ready to reject any 'outside' element because it does not fit some preconceived pattern. As Lenin puts it:

> We do not know and we cannot know which spark — out of the innumerable sparks that are scattering around in all countries as a result of the political and economic world crises — will kindle the conflagration, and therefore the most seemingly hopeless, musty and unfrequented directions are not to be taken for granted and overlooked, but diligently explored.

And so MacDiarmid lays special emphasis on the disparate element: on the discrete aspects of society, on the disruptive forces operating in it, for this kind of Marxist approach will be

> Rich in its discoveries of new problems,
> Important questions so far unsuspected,
> For which field research does not yet apply
> The data necessary to answer them.

This is indeed 'high, low, jack and the goddamn game'.

And what about the creative process, itself? Any good poem, of course, is constructed dialectically in the basic sense that it is the end-result, the synthesis, resulting from the interpenetration of form and content — or in a song from the wedding of words and melody — but the resultant felicity is not an accident, not a happy chance, but depends on how skilfully and how coolly the poet directs the operation. In the poem 'Utterly a Creator' MacDiarmid shows how cool and skilful, how clear-sighted and concentrated, the poet must be, how all gush and splurge rising from sense impressions, all 'irresponsible lyricism' must be ruthlessly eliminated. As a man he may love humanity but as a poet he must distance himself from everybody and everything which distracts him from his immediate task. For

> Only the irritations and icy ecstasies
> Of the artist's corrupted nervous system
> Are artistic — the very gift of style, form and expression

Is nothing else than this cool and fastidious attitude
Towards humanity . . . .

And so MacDiarmid bombards us with all the dialectical factors involved in the act of creation; idea and emotion, discipline and feeling, intellect and passion, germinal forces and living materials. And he gets a tremendous effect from this bombardment, a culminative effect which forces us to understand the process in which 'abrasive surfaces'

Are turned upon one another like millstones
And instead of generating chaos
Refine the grist of experience between them.

And we are immediately reminded of that beautiful, mysterious poem 'Crystals like Blood', which acts as a perfect poem-illustration of the process described, for in this poem which is concerned with his feelings for his dead wife, his living memory of her, we do find

The terrific and sustained impact
Of intellect upon passion and passion upon intellect

in a very strong direct form, and see how the 'grist of experience' has been most felicitously refined:

And feel once again released in me
The bright torrents of felicity, naturalness and faith
My treadmill memory draws from you yet.

But what about MacDiarmid himself? What are the special elements in his psyche which give rise to his poetry, his vision, his aesthetics? In 'The Task' he gives us a very frank, direct answer. He points to the 'gap or lacuna'

Between the innate and almost savage realism,
Which is a major element in my nature
And the imaginative, poetical cult
Whereby I have romanticised and idealised my life.

In other words the savage element leads to 'Ode to All Rebels' and the imaginative element to 'Song of the Seraphim'. Or do they? Perhaps it would be better to say the 'Song' represents the spirit of MacDiarmid and the 'Ode' the stamina. But does this take us any farther? A little, for spirit and stamina cannot be separated and this makes us doubtful if these two warring elements in his psyche really constitute a gap at all. MacDiarmid, as has been seen, is primarily interested in 'the interdependencies of life'. And these two elements are in fact the interdependencies of his own life. Distinct, separate and oppositional as they are, they still remain inter-dependent. Together they constitute a permanently frictional, self-correcting support system which is the motor-power of all his best work.

'Ode to all Rebels' is a most important poem in relation to the whole corpus of his work. The short extract given here is only part of a poem of some 800 lines which he assembled and re-assembled over a period of some fifteen years. The poem is blasphemous, anarchistic, destructive of all beliefs and belief-systems, and only the rebel, the outcast, the subversive element in man has any value:

> I am Ishmael, the only man
> Who's the friend of all men. . .
> I tell you all else is in vain.

This consciously subversive element is perhaps MacDiarmid's most important contribution to Marxist aesthetics. For many years in Marxist circles there has been very little discussion of 'the withering away of the State'. This most important idea of Marx, Engels and Lenin is after all the goal of Communism — the liberation of man and the spirit of man from repression by his fellow-man, the entry into the 'Realm of Freedom'. But too often this is forgotten by Marxists or relegated to some distant date in the future. The idea has become purely notional. And yet it is the most glorious idea that Communism has produced. And that is why MacDiarmid is a Communist. For him the 'withering away of the State' is not notional, it is the fundamental principle. As we see in 'Reflections in a Slum' it is not the poverty or the misery of the working class which draws his attention.

> Man does not cease to interest me
> When he ceases to be miserable.

It is their potential to transcend their own limitations and to come to full flower that commands his respect and solidarity, for, as he concludes:

> . . . *I am concerned with the blossom.*

And so MacDiarmid injects the subversive element, the withering-away process into his aesthetics right from the beginning. This ensures not an evolutionary development but a *permanently* revolutionary one, which constantly rejects the out-moded, constantly points to the new problems arising and leads to

> The calling out of the major images of the future
> What and as is — and as should and will be
> Reality in motion, advancing and developing.

But it is in 'Song of the Seraphim' that we get the fullest expression of the vision which animates his aesthetics and his poetry. The 'Song' is perhaps his most important poem because he is dealing with Life itself, as it is expressed in the whole age-long development of Man. It is a difficult poem, for the visionary is not easily grasped by us, limited as we are by time and space and materiality, and MacDiarmid's vision of 'what and as is — and as should and will be' extends beyond these limitations. And yet the poem itself is not mystical or obscure. It is in the form of a philosophical exposition, where each stage of the argument and counter-argument is fully spelled out and amply illustrated. Life in itself is incomprehensible but there is one factor that we can and must comprehend: the primordial urge of Life to overcome its own limitations, the driving necessity to abandon the old and out-moded and to seek constant renewal in higher and higher forms. This drive, this urge, this compelling necessity is reflected in Man and his society. And therefore the transfer from Capitalism to Socialism and from Socialism to Communism — and beyond — take on infinitely more important aspects than are commonly recognised. Man must mount a greater step higher 'than from the animal world to the world of man'.

> That, however is not technique
> Science, economics, organisation, learning
> Or any kind of reform or 'cleverness'.
> It is a *necessity* called for
> By the eternal primordial life . . .
> It is an act of the never-ending creation.

And here we begin to see the real connection between the 'Ode' and the 'Song'. The subversive element in the 'Ode' is the individual, tactical expression of the poet concerned with the 'interdependences of life', while the 'Song' expresses the eternal strategy of Life itself.

> I tell you all else is in vain.

This great vision of Life and Civilisation which MacDiarmid has compels him to give an urgent, fundamental warning to the Communist world and to Socialists everywhere. The establishment of Socialism must be completely revolutionary. Its purpose must be much greater than merely satisfying material needs. The working class will fail in its historical mission if it overthrows the bourgeoisie — only to become a new bourgeoisie, itself, with a smattering of Philistine art and education to disguise its true character. Socialism must rid itself of all bourgeois ideology, of all elements of statism and Philistinism. It must create a new need, the need to advance to Communism and 'the Realm of Freedom', and it must enlist the whole-hearted support of creative artists (poets, writers) everywhere for they are not primarily concerned with 'satiety' and 'well-being' but with fundamental spiritual development. And it is they who must give expression to

> That higher and stronger quickening life
> We seek eternally and to-day
> Must discover anew
> Eternally transcends the objective spirit
> Because it has nothing objective,
> Only life.

And only in this way can man fully respond to 'the call of the Seraphim', to the eternal strategy of Life itself. Only in this way can we attain to the 'Supreme', to the highest form of Man, to the high season of Civilisation, where the cortex and the thalamus work in harmony, where mind, will, psyche and spirit

> All identical, all separate, and all united are life.

This brief survey of MacDiarmid's poetry and aesthetics is limited since it is based on only a small portion of his total work, but hopefully it gives some idea of the greatness of the man and casts extra light not only on his Socialist poems but on the whole range of his poetry at large. It is also intended as a challenge to Marxist critics everywhere, and especially to those in the Socialist countries, to come to grips with MacDiarmid in all his complexity, so that a full evaluation of his work can become available to readers all over the world.

As for Scotland, he is the greatest poet our country has ever produced and he stands with John MacLean as one of the two great Scotsmen of the twentieth century. It can truly be said of MacDiarmid, as he himself said of MacLean, that

MacDiarmid, too, is 'krassivy, krassivy', the magic word which means both beautiful and red:

> For I am corn and not chaff, and will neither
> Be blown away by the wind, nor burst with the flail,
> But will abide them both
> And in the end prevail.

T.S.L.
T.B.

1

THE BONNIE BROUKIT BAIRN

(For Peggy)

Mars is braw in crammasy,
Venus in a green silk goun,
The auld mune shak's her gowden feathers,
Their starry talk's a wheen o' blethers,
Nane for thee a thochtie sparin',
Earth, thou bonnie broukit bairn!
—But greet, an' in your tears ye'll droun
The haill clanjamfrie!

2

MY CLAN IS DARKNESS

My clan is darkness 'yont a wee ring
O' memory showin' catsiller here or there
But nocht complete or lookin' twice the same.
Graham, Murray, Carruthers, Frater, and faur mair
Auld Border breeds than I can tell ha' been
        Woven in its skein.

Great hooses keep their centuried lines complete.
Better than I can mind my faither they
Preserve their forbears painted on their wa's
And can trace ilka tendency and trait
O' bluid and spirit in their divers stages
        Doon the ages.

To mind and body I ha' nae sic clue,
A water flowin' frae an unkent source
Wellin' up in me to catch the licht at last
At this late break in its hidden course.
Yet my blin' instincts nurtured in the dark
        Sing sunwards like the lark.

broukit, neglected   bairn, child   braw, handsome
crammasy, crimson   wheen o' blethers, pack of nonsense
greet, weep   clanjamfrie, collection
catsiller, mica   ilka, every

I canna signal to a single soul
In a' the centuries that led up to me
In happy correspondence, yet to a'
These nameless thanks for strength and cleanness gi'e,
And mair, auld Border breeds, ken I inherit,
    And croun, your frontier spirit.

Reivers to weavers and to me. Weird way!
Yet in the last analysis I've sprung
Frae battles, mair than ballads, and it seems
The thrawn auld water has at last upswung
Through me, and's mountin' like the vera devil
    To its richt level!

3

CROWDIEKNOWE

Oh to be at Crowdieknowe
When the last trumpet blaws,
An' see the deid come loupin' owre
The auld grey wa's.

Muckle men wi' tousled beards
I grat at as a bairn
'll scramble frae the croodit clay
Wi' feck o' swearin'.

An' glower at God an' a' His gang
O' angels i' the lift
— Thae trashy bleezin' French-like folk
Wha gar'd them shift!

Fain the weemun-folk'll seek
To mak' them haud their row
— Fegs, God's no blate gin he stirs up
The men o' Crowdieknowe!

reivers, freebooters   thrawn, obstinate
loupin', jumping   muckle, big   grat, cried
croodit, crowded   feck, plenty   lift, sky
fain, eagerly   blate, backward

4

WHY I CHOOSE RED

I fight in red for the same reasons
That Garibaldi chose the red shirt
— Because a few men in a field wearing red
Look like many men — if there are ten you will think
There are a hundred; if a hundred
You will believe them a thousand.
And the colour of red dances in the enemy's rifle sights
And his aim will be bad — But, best reason of all,
A man in a red shirt can neither hide nor retreat.

5

SEPARATISM

If there's a sword-like sang
That can cut Scotland clear
O' a' the warld beside
Rax me the hilt o't here,

For there's nae jewel till
Frae the rest o' earth it's free,
Wi' the starry separateness
I'd fain to Scotland gie. . . .

6

UNCONSCIOUS GOAL OF HISTORY

Unconscious goal of history, dimly seen
In Genius whiles that kens the problem o' its age.
And works at it; the mass o' men pursue
Their puir blind purposes unaware o' you,
And yet frae them emerges tae your keen
Clear consequences nae man can gauge

Save in relation to some ancient stage;
Sae History mak's the ambitions o' great men
Means to ends greater than themsels could ken,
—Greater and ither—and mass ignorance yields,
Like corruption o' vegetation in fallow fields,
The conditions o' richer increase;—at last
The confusion's owre, the time comes fast
When men wauk to the possibility
O' workin' oot and makin, their destiny
In fu' consciousness and cease to muddle through
Wi' nae idea o' their goal—and nae mair grue!

Let nane cry that the right men arena here
—That urgent tasks await that nane can dae.
Times oft mistak' their problems in that way.
At the richt time the richt men aye appear.
If Scotland fills us wi' despair we may
Be proposin' a goal that disna lie
Onywhaur in history's plan the noo; we sigh
In vain—because we canna think in vain
And oor desire'll hae its due effect
In the lang run altho' oor age rejects.
But a'e thing's certain—nae genius'll come,
Nae maitter hoo he's shouted for, to recreate
The life and fabric o' a decadent State
That's dune its work, gien its Idea to the world,
The problem is to find in Scotland some
Bricht coil o' you that hasna yet uncurled,
And, hoosoever petty I may be, the fact
That I think Scotland isna dune yet proves
There's something in it that fulfilment's lacked
And my vague hope through a' creation moves.

The Unconscious Ideas that impel a race
Spring frae an ineffable sense o' hoo to be
A certain kind o' human being—Let's face
This fact in Scotland and we'll see
The fantasy o' an unconquerable soul
Neath nations' rivalries, persecutions, wars,
The golden casket o' their Covenant, their goal,
Shrined in a dwelling that ootshines the stars,
A dwelling o' delight no' made wi' hands,

nae mair grue, no more revulsion

For wha's sake till the gaen oot o' the Sun
They'll hew the Sassenach, the Amalekite, the Hun
Nor sacrifice the least fraction o' their will
To independence while they've a tittle still
O' their Unconscious Idea unrealised.
Is Scotland roupit that I su'd gie owre
My quest for onything, hooso'er disguised,
That wi' a new vitality may endower
My thieveless country: and mak' it mair
Intelligently allied to your hidden purpose there
Sae that my people frae their living graves
May loup and play a pairt in History yet
Wi' sufferin's mair like a Genius's than a slave's.
Vieve strands in your endless glories knit?
By thocht a man mak's his idea a force
Or fact in History's drama: He canna foresee
The transformations and uses o' the course
The dialectics o' human action and interaction'll gie
The contribution he mak's—it'll a' depend
On his sincerity and clearness in the end
And his integrity—his unity with you;
Strivin' to gie birth to that idea through
Him wha o' makin' his meanin' clear
May weel despair when you disappear—or appear.
Stir me, Cencrastus. If the faintest gleam
O' you kyths in my work fu' weel I ken
That your neist movement may lowse a supreme
Glory—tho' I'm extinguished then!

roupit, auctioned thieveless, purposeless vieve, vivid
Cencrastus, the curly snake (ancient Celtic symbol of wisdom)
kyths, appears lowse, set loose

7

THE GLEN OF SILENCE

By this cold shuddering fit of fear
My heart divines a presence here,
Goddess or ghost yclept;
Wrecker of homes . . .

Where have I heard a silence before
Like this that only a lone bird's cries
And the sound of a brawling burn to-day
Serve in this wide empty glen but to emphasize?

Every doctor knows it—the stillness of foetal death,
The indescribable silence over the abdomen then!
A silence literally 'heard' because of the way
It stands out in the auscultation of the abdomen.

Here is an identical silence, picked out
By a bickering burn and a lone bird's wheeple
—The foetal death in this great 'cleared' glen
Where the *fear-tholladh nan tighean* has done his foul work
—The tragedy of an unevolved people.

8

BALLAD OF THE GENERAL STRIKE

I saw a rose come loupin' oot
Frae a camsteerie plant.
O wha'd ha'e thocht yon puir stock had
Sic an inhabitant?

For centuries it ran to waste,
Wi' pin-heid flooers at times.
O'ts hidden hert o' beauty they
Were but the merest skimes.

fear-tholladh nan tighean, destroyer of homes
camsteerie, perverse   skimes, glimmers

Yet while it ran to wud and thorns,
The feckless growth was seekin'
Some airt to cheenge its life until
A' in a rose was beekin'.

'Is there nae way in which my life
Can mair to flooerin' come,
And bring its waste on shank and jags
Doon to a minimum?

'It's hard to struggle as I maun
For scrunts o' blooms like mine,
While blossom covers ither plants
As by a knack divine.

'What hinders me unless I lack
Some needfu' discipline?
—I wis I'll bring my orra life
To beauty or I'm din!'

Sae ran the thocht that hid ahint
The thistle's ugsome guise,
'I'll brak' the habit o' my life
A worthier to devise.

'My nobler instincts sall nae mair
This contrair shape be gi' en.
I sall nae mair consent to live
A life no' fit to be seen.'

Sae ran the thocht that hid ahint
The thistle's ugsome guise,
Till a' at aince a rose loupt oot
—I watched it wi' surprise.

A rose loupt oot and grew, until
It was ten times the size
O' ony rose the thistle afore
Hed heistit to the skies.

wud, would airt, way beekin', showing scrunts, stunted things
wis, know ugsome, ugly hed heistit, had hoisted

And still it grew till a' the buss
Was hidden in its flame.
I never saw sae braw a floo'er
As yon thrawn stock became.

And still it grew until it seemed
The haill braid earth had turned
A reid reid rose that in the lift
Like a ball o' fire burned.

The waefu' clay was fire aince mair,
As Earth had been resumed
Into God's mind, frae which sae lang
To grugous state 'twas doomed.

Syne the rose shrivelled suddenly
As a balloon is burst;
The thistle was a ghaistly stick,
As gin it had been curst.

Was it the ancient vicious sway
Imposed itsel' again,
Or nerve owre weak for new emprise
That made the effort vain,

A coward strain in that lorn growth
That wrocht the sorry trick?
—The thistle like a rocket soared
And cam' doon like the stick.

Like grieshuckle the roses glint,
The leafs like farles hing,
As roond a hopeless sacrifice
Earth draws its barren ring.

The dream o' beauty's dernin' yet
Ahint the ugsome shape.
—Vain dream that in a pinheid here
And there can e'er escape!

buss, bush thrawn, obstinate
grugous, ugly grieshuckle, embers farles, ash filaments
dernin', hiding

The vices that defeat the dream
Are in the plant itsel',
And till they're purged its virtues maun
In pain and misery dwell.

Let Deils rejoice to see the waste,
The fond hope brocht to nocht.
The thistle in their een is as
A favourite lust they've wrocht.

The orderin' o' the thistle means
Nae richtin' o't to them.
Its loss they ca' a law, its thorns
A fule's fit diadem.

And still the idiot nails itsel'
To its ain crucifix,
While here a rose and there a rose
Jaups oot abune the pricks.

Like connoisseurs the Deils gang roond
And praise its attitude,
Till on the Cross the silly Christ
To fidge fu' fain's begood!

Like connoisseurs the Deils gang roond
Wi' ready platitude.
It's no' sae dear as vinegar,
And every bit as good!

The bitter taste is on my tongue,
I chowl my chafts, and pray
'Let God forsake me noo and no'
Staund connoisseur-like tae!' . . .

Deils, Devils
jaups, splashes   fidge fu' fain's begood, has begun to move eagerly
chowl my chafts, distort my jaws

The language that but sparely flooers
And maistly gangs to weed;
The thocht o' Christ and Calvary
Aye liddenin' in my heid;
And a' the dour provincial thocht
That merks the Scottish breed
—These are the thistle's characters,
To argie there'e nae need.
Hoo weel my verse embodies
The thistle you can read!
—But will a Scotsman never
Frae this vile growth be freed? . . .

9

BEHIND THE SYMBOLS

Let the hearts of my people be lifted up
Once more with the daily sight
Of an eagle wheeling on majestic vans
That is our Scottish birthright.

Fill their lives again with the noblest form
At liberty in Europe still—
The red stag pausing with lifted hoof
On the sun-assailing hill.

For these are among Earth's glorious symbols
To souls of men needing symbols yet
And a man must be well nourished on these
To embrace the Infinite.

But the supreme spirit enters into all
As an otter into its watery home
As if without dividing its flow
And making no ripple, bubble, or foam.

Even so in the course of time I hope
My people will open their hearts until
They are like the lochs the hill-streams feed
Forever—but cannot overspill.

liddenin', moving to and fro

10

TO HELL WI' HAPPINESS

To hell wi' happiness!
I sing the terrifyin' discipline
O' the free mind that gars a man
Make his joys kill his joys,
The weakest by the strongest,
The temporal by the fundamental
(Or hope o' the fundamental)
And prolong wi'in himself
Threids o' thocht sae fragile
It needs the help and continuance
O' a' his vital power
To haud them frae brakin'
As he pou's them owre the gulfs.
Oor humanity canna follow us
To lichts sae faur removed.
A man ceases to be himsel'
Under sicna constraint.
Will he find life or daith
At the end of his will,
At thocht's deepest depth,
Or some frightfu' sensation o' seein'
Nocht but the ghastly glimmer
O' his ain puir maitter?
  What does it maitter?
  It's the only road,
The beaten track is *beaten* frae the stert.

Man's the reality that mak's
A' thing possible, even himsel'!
Energy's his miracle,
But hoo little he's dune wi't yet,
Denyin't at ilka turn.
Ilka change has Eternity's mandate.
But hoo little we've changed since Adam!

gars, makes   ilka, every   wi't, with it

11

WITH THE HERRING FISHERS

'I see herrin'.'—I hear the glad cry
And 'gainst the moon see ilka blue jowl
In turn as the fishermen haul on the nets
And sing: 'Come, shove in your heids and growl.

'Soom on, bonnie herrin', soom on,' they shout,
Or 'Come in, O come in, and see me,'
'Come gie the auld man something to dae.
It'll be a braw change frae the sea.'

O it's ane o' the bonniest sichts in the warld
To watch the herrin' come walkin' on board
In the wee sma' 'oors o' a simmer's morning'
As if o' their ain accord.

For this is the way that God sees life,
The haill jing-bang o's appearin'
Up owre frae the edge o' naethingness
—It's his happy cries I'm hearin'.

'Left, right—O come in and see me',
Reid and yellow and black and white
Toddlin' up into Heaven thegither
At peep o' day frae the endless night.

'I see herring',' I hear his glad cry,
And 'gainst the moon see his muckle blue jowl,
As he handles buoy-tow and bush-raip
Singin': 'Come, shove in your heids and growl!'

ilka, every soom, swim dae, do braw, fine
wee sma' 'oors, the early hours simmer, summer
haill jing-bang o's, the whole collection of us thegither, together
buoy-tow, buoy rope bush-raip, rope attached to net

12

POETRY AND PROPAGANDA

It is no doubt a natural ambition
And even perhaps a worthy one
For a poet to have his genius hailed
In seeming mounting triumphs won
Till the so-called greatest of the land
Are proud to take him by the hand.

But once he stands among them
Their peer, and more; and all
The exclusive portals gladly
Wide open to him fall
Let him in no vain pleasure reel
But only rising nausea feel.

His place is not with lords and ladies
And millionaires and learned men
Enough to prove himself among them,
And turn his back upon them then
And join the people among whom
Alone the Muse's wings have room.

Name any of the accounted great.
Who can imagine any worthy song
Addressed in compliment to such
Or allied to exploitation and social wrong?—
But any down-and-out can test and tax
The mightiest pinions—or wings of wax!

Propaganda in poetry let humbugs condemn
But slavery none can extol to-day
Nor chant in favour of charming wage-cuts
Nor sing of tyranny's bracing sway
And half our poetlings still laud in verse
Will be equally out of the question ere long.

True they do not sing of sound finance
Or praise wage-slavery openly—
But a turn in affairs and they voice
Blood-lust and theft unashamedly;
And all the sweet sentiments they fear to express
Lie hidden in their lines none the less.

A pretty tribute to the old rural scene
Can mask a base betrayal of mankind;
The mellowest religious reference conceal
The Kruschen spirit of Fascism behind,
In short, any utterance that is not pure
Propaganda is impure propaganda for sure!

13

REFLECTIONS IN AN IRONWORKS

Would you resembled the metal you work with,
Would the iron entered into your souls,
Would you became like steel on your own behalf!
You are still only putty that tyranny rolls
Between its fingers! You makers of bayonets and guns
For your own destruction! No wonder that those
Weapons you make turn on you and mangle and murder—
You fools who equip your otherwise helpless foes!

14

IN THE CHILDREN'S HOSPITAL

'Does it matter? Losing your legs?'
Siegfried Sassoon

Now let the legless boy show the great lady
How well he can manage his crutches.
It doesn't matter though the Sister objects,
'He's not used to them yet,' when such is
The will of the Princess. Come, Tommy,
Try a few desperate steps through the ward.
Then the hand of Royalty will pat your head
And life suddenly cease to be hard.
For a couple of legs are surely no miss
When the loss leads to such an honour as this!
One knows, when one sees how jealous the rest
Of the children are, it's been all for the best!—
But would the sound of your sticks on the floor
Thundered in her skull for evermore!

15

DIE GRENZSITUATION

Was *this* the face that launched a thousand ships?
No! But it frightened one right smartly down the slips
When—while the whole world held its silly breath—
She gave it her own holy name—as sure as death!
Deeming *that* the greatest compliment that she,
After a profound spell of Queenly secrecy,
To duty nobly yielding her notorious modesty,
Could pay this miracle of Clydeside industry,
And everybody (almost!) hastened to agree
And marvelled how she'd got the great idea,
Perfect, sublime, the very peak of poetry,
An epic in three words, *The Queen Mary*,
And not one honest soul in Glasgow, or Christendom, laughed!
It seemed—and was—as though she'd stricken all mankind daft.

16

ROYAL WEDDING GIFTS

It is unfortunately understandable enough
That gifts should pour in from all over the earth:
Not so the greed of the girl who accepts so much
And so monstrously overrates her own scant worth.

The daughter of a base and brainless breed
Is given what countless better women sorely need,
But cannot get one ten-millionth part of tho' they
    slave and save
Relentlessly from the cradle to the grave.

Rope in the shameless hussy—let her be
Directed to factory work or domestic service
Along with all the other spivs and drones—
Our life-stream's clogged and fouled with all these
    damned convervas.

17

PLASTER MADONNA

In the baptistry of a village Church in the Pyrenees
An Anarchist militiaman said to me
'This damned junk'—and he pointed
To the charred and tumbled mummery before the church—
'Is still *alive* in the minds of many of our people.
Once, perhaps, it comforted them.
Now it is just a lingering and shadowy fear.'
He told me a legend from his own town, Arenys de Mar.
The people of Arenys commissioned a statue of the Virgin
From a famous image maker of Palma de Majorca.
A tremendous storm arose soon after
The statue-bearing ship had left Palma Bay,
And not all the prayers and entreaties of the crew
Could secure divine help against the storm.
Suddenly one of the seamen understood
What had happened — and rushing to the box

In which the image was packed, he turned it over,
Whereupon the storm went down.
The Virgin had been laid face downward
And to express her displeasure
Had raised the storm.
How charming, you say, a fine, dramatic, mediaeval legend!
No such thing. In Arenys the old women will tell you
The date of that storm. It was 1861.
Do you begin to see the truth in the Anarchist's statement—
That minds whose imaginations are controlled
By a culture of this type
Can never hope to live happily
In a world that has placed
New techniques and new responsibilities
In people's hands? Gad, sir,
That seaman's 'understanding' of the trouble
Is precisely all the 'understanding'
Of the Right ever amounts to.

18

AFTER TWO THOUSAND YEARS

The Christians have had two thousand years
And what have they done?—
Made the bloodiest and beastliest world ever seen
Under the sun.

No Christian refuses to profit himself
From his brother's misfortune.
The devil who would sup with our Christian banks
Must sup with a hellish long spoon.

The Christian Churches are all built up
In utter defiance of all Christ taught.
Co-religionists war at home and abroad,
Each side supported by the self-same God.

And blandly the Bishops bestow their blessings
On any murderer or fraud with the wit
To pay them, lip-serve the Cross, and keep
The working-classes carrying it.

19

THE ALL-SCOTLAND SALVATION STAMPEDE

The brash illiteracy—the use of the Bible as a rag-bag of texts, to be learned by heart, the preacher who brandishes a wheel on whose hub and circumference 'Christ' is written, and spells out the word c-h-u-r-c-h, saying 'Take U away, and it's meaningless: this means U are needed.'
—Press

Survey most nations and most ages. Examine the religious principles which have, in fact, prevailed in the world. You will scarcely be persuaded that they are anything but sick men's dreams. Or perhaps will regard them more as the playsome whimsies of monkeys in human shape than the serious, positive asservations of a being who dignifies himself with the name of rational. — David Hume

What about Dr Billy Graham and all
The 'Tell Scotland' parsons today who call
Our fatuous folk back to the Bible story
Equating ignorance and superstition with glory?
What about the hordes of mindless fans who tryst
In the same way with a crooner, a film star, Churchill,
  Attlee, or Christ?

By every movement of their facial features,
By every word and gesture, these creatures
Declare their ardent and boundless devotion
To the great ideas and interests that reach their lug
With precisely the same emotion
As Persian camomile inspires in a bug!*

* With acknowledgments to Dmitri Pisarev (1810-68).

20

A POINT IN TIME

Now you understand how stars and hearts are one with another
And how there can nowhere be an end, nowhere a hindrance;
How the boundless dwells perfect and undivided in the spirit,
How each part can be infinitely great, and infinitely small,
How the utmost extension is but a point, and how
Light, harmony, movement, power
All identical, all separate, and all united are life.

21

CONCEPTION

I have reached the stage when questioning myself
Concerning the love of Scotland and turning inward
Upon my own spirit, there comes to me
The suggestion of something utterly unlike
All that is commonly meant by loving
One's country, one's brother man, not altruism,
Not kindly feeling, not outward-looking sympathy,
But something different from all these,
Something almost awful in its range,
Its rage and fire, its scope and height and depth,
Something growing up, within my own
Separate and isolated lonely being,
Within the deep dark of my own consciousness,
Flowering in my own heart, my own self
(Not the Will to Power, but the Will to Flower!)
So that indeed I could not be myself
Without this strange, mysterious, awful finding
Of my people's very life within my own
—This terrible blinding discovery
Of Scotland in me, and I in Scotland,
Even as a man, loyal to a man's code and outlook,
Discovers within himself woman alive and eloquent,
Pulsing with her own emotion,
Looking out on the world with her own vision.

22

LOURD ON MY HERT

Lourd on my hert as winter lies
The state that Scotland's in the day.
Spring to the North has aye come slow
But noo dour winter's like to stay
    For guid,
    An no' for guid!

O wae's me on the weary days
When it is scarce grey licht at noon;
It maun be a' the stupid folk
Diffusin' their dullness roon and roon
    Like soot
    That keeps the sunlicht oot.

Nae wonder if I think I see
A lichter shadow than the neist
I'm fain to cry: 'The dawn, the dawn!
I see it brakin' in the East.'
    But ah
    —It's juist mair snaw!

23

EDINBURGH TOUN

O Edinburgh toun, Edinburgh toun,
Police are setting steel-boxes roun
To shoot the workin'-classes doun
Under a Chief Constable—Whoa, horsie, steady!—
Juist the spit-image o' 'Peacemaker' Neddy.

lourd, heavy   dour, hard, grim   guid, good   neist, next

24

EDINBURGH

Most of the denizens wheeze, sniffle, and
exude a sort of snozzling whnoff whnoff,
apparently through a hydrophile sponge.
Ezra Pound

The capital of Scotland is called Auld Reekie,
Signifying a monstrous acquiescence
In the domination of the ends
By the evidences of effort.
—Not the mastery of matter
By the spirit of man
But, at best, a damnable draw,
A division of the honours
And, far more, the dishonours!
—Dark symbol of a society
Of 'dog eat dog'.
Under which the people reveal themselves to the world
Completely naked in their own skin,
Like toads!
Yes, see, the dead snatch at the living here.
So the social corpse, the dead class,
The dead mode of life, the dead religion,
Have an after life as vampires.
They are not still in their graves
But return among us.
They rise with the fumes
From the chimney of the crematorium
And again settle down on the earth
And cover it with black filth.

To repossess ourselves of the primal power
'Let there be light' and apply it
In our new, how ever more complex, setting
Is all. And let us not cry
'Too difficult! Impossible!' forgetting
That the stupendous problems that obsess us to-day
Are as nothing to the problems overcome
By the miraculous achievements of men in the past
—Yes, the first problems in the very dawn of human history
Were infinitely greater, and our troubles are due

To the fact that we have largely lost
The earliest, the most essential,
The *distinctively human* power
Our early ancestors had in abundant measure
Whatever else they lacked that we possess.
Possess thanks to them!—and thanks to the primal
   indispensable power
They had and we have lost progressively
And affect to despise—
Fools who have lost the substance
And cling to the shadow.
Auld Reekie indeed!
Preferring darkness rather than light
Because our deeds are evil!
I see the dark face of an early mother of men
By a primitive campfire of history.
Her appearance is rendered all the more remarkable
Because of the peculiar performance of the smoke.
By some process, natural no doubt but mysterious to us,
She exercises a strange control over the smoke
As she shuffles round—with vast protruding lips
And with wide rings hanging from her ears,
Weaving her hands. And it is
As if the billows of thick white vapour
Are forced to follow her will
And make a magical dancing cloud
Behind her as she moves.
Learn again to consume your own smoke like this,
Edinburgh, to free your life from the monstrous pall,
To subdue it and be no longer subdued by it,
Like the hand of the dyer in his vat.
So all the darkness of industrialism yet
Must be relegated like a moth that pursues
The onward dance of humanity.

So the mighty impetus of creative force
That seeks liberation, that shows even through
The scum of swinish filth of bourgeois society,
The healthy creative force will break through
—Even in Edinburgh—and good, human things grow,
Protecting and justifying faith
In regeneration to a free and noble life
When labour shall be a thing
Of honour, valour, and heroism

And 'civilization' no longer like Edinburgh
On a Sabbath morning,
Stagnant and foul with the rigid peace
Of an all-tolerating frigid soul!

This is the great skill that mankind has lost.
The distinctively human power.
Lo! A poor negress teaches this rich university city
Something more important than all it knows,
More valuable than all it has!
But Edinburgh—Edinburgh—is too stupid yet
To learn how not to stand in her own light.

25

HOSTINGS OF HEROES

There are two days, two sights, I covet most
Of all in the depths of our history lost.

First, Clontarf, where, says the Irish annalist,*
Earl Sigurd in person led into battle
The wild men from the Orc Islands and the Cat Islands,
From Manaan and Sci and Leodus,
From Ceinn-Tire and from airir-gaidhed,
And 'an immense army' from the Innis-Gall.

Next, that glorious scene when Dundee
Sent out the Fiery Cross, and the Chiefs
Met him in their war array,
Like the muster of the war-chiefs in the Iliad
As John Philip portrays it in his epic (in Latin)—†
The divers branches of Clan Donald, all with tufts
Of heather tied to their spear-heads, and each
Under its own chieftains
—Black Alasdair of Glengarry, young Clanranald,

* Battle of Clontarf, 1014.

† The epic *The Grameid* has been published, with a translation, by the Scottish History Society.

Glencoe huge as a giant, with his twisted beard
Curled backward, and his wild eyes rolling,
And Keppoch in gilded armour,
The two Macleans, Duart and Otter,
Macleod of Raasay, in the old Highland dress
Of saffron shirt, belted plaid, and rawhide shoes,
Raasay who could outstrip the deer
And take the wild bull by the horns and master him,
Young Stuart of Appin, MacNaughton of Dundarave,
Grant of Glenmoriston, MacAlaster of Loup, and a host of others,
And above all, Lochiel, the old Ulysses
—A helmet covers his head
A double-edged brand is girt to his side.
Blood-red plumes float on his crest,
A cuirass of leather, harder than adamant,
Girds his breast—on his left arm hangs his shield.
His tartan hose are gartered round his calf,
Mail covers his shoulders
And a brazen plate his back.
His very look, so fierce,
Might fright the boldest foe,
His savage glance, the swarthy hue
Of his Spanish countenance, his flashing eyes,
His beard and moustache
Curled like the moon's horns.

But in the place of all this
What have we to-day?
Dingy parades of vermin!
Details of the English army
In clothes the colour of excrement;
Or processions like that in Edinburgh
In honour of Sir Walter Scott's centenary,
A funeral trickle of Bailies and Lawyers,
Members of the Leith Water Board,
And, sole representative of the Republic of Letters,
Hugh Walpole!

God! What a crawl of cockroaches!

26

THE BLACK GUARDS

Yea, and with, and because of all this, the poetry
For which the poet at any moment may be smashed to pulp
By a gang of educated chimpanzees
Beating out the scansion with a rubber truncheon
For metronome on the small of his back
Till his kidneys burst—the poetry,
Not in Germany and certain other countries only,
But everywhere, England, Scotland, America,
The poetry of War and Civil War everywhere,
The poetry of the world-wide Night of the Long Knives
In which 99 men in every 100 are Gestapo Guards,
The poetry that entails the Family Trial
Of the poet's wife and children too,
And makes hulking Black Guards seize the Muses,
Tie their clothing tightly above their heads,
Truss, blind, shamefully humiliate them.
The Black Guards are among the helpless Muses now,
Beating them with clubs, kicking them in the guts,
The Black Guards carry on their dastardly work
While splitting their sides with laughter,
The Black Guards—Finance, Religion, Law, Capitalist Culture.
Himmler never moves a muscle—shows no pity
When, on his departure, frightful screams from the
        parade-ground
Tell of the most shameful deeds of all. . . .Next day
Ladies he meets at State functions
Are charmed by his quiet courtesy.
The poetry that is scheduled as a Dangerous Occupation,
The most dangerous occupation in the world to-day.
. . . .Locked in a cell with a Luger pistol
I make my poetry of World Consciousness.
But will any of it ever be smuggled out
From the Sondergericht to which all Consciouness is subject
All over the world to-day?

27

FASCISTS, YOU HAVE KILLED MY COMRADES

(A Poem written during the Spanish War, with two verses written by way of a postscript two years later.)

Fascists, you have killed my comrades
And their wives and children!
You have killed them!
It were better that you should all rot in your vices,
In the bottomless filth of damnation,
And that they should live!
What is the worth of your plague-spotted lives
That such a price should be paid for them?
But it is too late — too late!
I cry aloud, but they do not hear me.
I beat the doors of the graves
But they will not wake.
Take your victory — I fling it to you as a bone
Is flung to a pack of snarling curs.
The price of your banquet is paid for you.
Come then and gorge yourselves,
Cannibals, blood-suckers, carrion beasts
That feed on the dead!
This is the body that was given for you
—Look at it, torn and bleeding,
Throbbing still with the tortured life,
Quivering from the bitter death-agony!
Take it, Christians, and eat.
'All Spain', it has been said of Goya,
'Is in the volume and range of his work.'
—That is true. Even *you* are there,
But not in the *Vendimia* — only in the terrible painting
of *The Executions After the Dos de Mayo*,
Napoleon's soldiers firing on a group of unarmed civilians,
That—and the people dead of hunger, guns, and pestilence;
The twisted zeal of the Inquisition,
The hag-ridden mythology of the peninsula
And the pretty, distracting duchesses —
Is all that you know and have and are
Of Goya and of Spain.

Postscript

Ah, Spain, already your tragic landscapes
And the agony of your war to my mind appear
As tears may come into the eyes of a woman very slowly
So slowly as to leave them CLEAR!
Spain! The International Brigade! At the moment it seems
As though the pressure of a loving hand had gone,
The touch under which my close-pressed fingers seemed to thrill
And the skin to divide up into little zones
Of heat and cold whose position continually changed
So that the whole of my hand, held in that clasp,
Was in a state of internal movement.
My hands that were full of love
Are empty again. . . .for a while,
For a little while!

28

IN MEMORIAM GARCIA LORCA

Lorca! 'Pensive, merry, and dear to the people
As a guitar, simple-hearted and responsive as a child
—His whole life was helpful and inspiring to others
And he earned his people's deep and lasting affection.'*
Lorca's love of his people, clear in his writings,
Met with a passionate response. His songs and ballads
Were quickly caught up all over revolutionary Spain.
The Fascist henchmen could never forgive
His popularity and devotion to the people.
They shot him and made a bonfire of his books
On Carmen Square in Granada.
'Fear not! This debt we shall repay!'†
Lorca's poetry, however, can never be silenced.
It will continue to blow as free as the wind
Over the wide spaces of heroic Spain.
Lorca, dead, lives forever.

* From Pablo Neruda's tribute to Lorca.
† From lines addressed to Lorca by Chris de Topia.

The poet has been turned into earth and silence,
Yet every day he dies and resuscitates in the heart of Spain,
In the heart of the world, because today the world
Bleeds and throbs together with the people of Spain
—Angel Lazaro is right when he cries:
'How was it that the murderers' bullets did not stop
Before that brow
Below which the angels of verse
Sang a matchless music?'
I think of that head struck to the ground
The black lock fallen as though it wanted to go
With the last stertor
To the thread of recondite water
Of his Andalusia.
I think of Lorca dead—he who stood upright
In the middle of life
Like a young bull in the middle of the fields.
I think of the last terror of his pupils,
Those pupils that had known how to see
Unique colours and foreshortenings of wonder,
And thinking of that
I cannot utter any word but this:
Murderers! Murderers!

29

IN THE GANGS

Gangs of louts at every street corner
Full of nothing but *ochiania.* *

True, they are keenly aware of their sensation
But is not this sensory awareness
The most elementary form of consciousness.

* Russian word, meaning no-belief, no love, no fear.

On the other hand they cannot be said
To think at all, and their feelings are rather
Sharp transitory reactions
Than long-continued dominant emotions.
Above all, they are devoid of will and purpose,
Helplessly impelled hither and yon by the
circumstances of the moment.

They have no strength of resistance. They are weak
At the very core of personality. . . the power to choose,
Freedom of choice may be an illusion
But if so it is an inescapable one.
When the mainspring of choice is weakened or left out
The conflicts and contradictions of character
Lose their virtue and significance
And personality almost disappears.
They are hardly persons enough to sustain
Real relations with one another
Any more than billiard balls do.

30

JOY IN THE TWENTIETH CENTURY

Life isn't so bad, life isn't so bad,
No matter what the pessimists say.
Every now and again the general heart
Goes up like a lark soaring light and gay.

Life isn't so bad, life isn't so bad.
Unstop your ears and you'll hear the glad cries
Of hundreds of thousands of men and their families.—
To-day the Railwaymen get a twopenny rise!

It seems as though the very sun
Has multiplied itself. A penny had been
Great tidings; whole twopence is enough
To dazzle the entire terrestrial scene.

AND, ABOVE ALL, MY POETRY IS MARXIST

The greatest poets undergo a kind of crisis in their art,
A change proportionate to their previous achievement.
Others approach it and fail to fulfil it—like Wordsworth.
Some, like Keats, the crisis helps to kill.
Rimbaud underwent a normal, not an abnormal, poetic crisis.
What was abnormal was his extreme youth, his circumstances,
his peasant stock.
It killed Keats, but Keats was not born of French peasants.
It kept Milton practically silent for twenty years.
Rimbaud died at the end of nineteen. Yet he explored it seems
After his own manner an even more hidden way.
Claudel said that, after reading him, he felt
'L' impression vivante et presque physique de surnaturel. . .
Il n'était pas de ce monde.' The priest who confessed him
Said to his sister: 'I have rarely met a faith
Of the quality of his.' That was not to be taken
(As his sister took it) in any easy pious sense;
He remained very much *de ce monde.*
But it seems that through these years
He walked in granite within and without,
And perhaps only his poetry had not found
—And he but thirty-seven—
A method of being which was, for him,
What he desired, perdurable as the granite.
—I am forty-six; of tenacious, long-lived, country folk.
Fools regret my poetic change—from my 'enchanting early lyrics'
But I have found in Marxism all that I need—
(I on my mother's side of long-lived Scottish peasant stock
And on my father's of hardy keen-brained Border mill-workers)
It only remains to perfect myself in this new mode.
This is the poetry I want—all
I can regard now as poetry at all,
As poetry of to-day, not of the past,
A Communist poetry that bases itself
On the Resolution of the C.C. of the R.C.P.
In Spring 1925: 'The Party must vigorously oppose
Thoughtless and contemptuous treatment
Of the old cultural heritage
As well as of the literary specialists. . . .
It must likewise combat the tendency
Towards a purely hothouse proletarian literature.

32

THE BELLY-GRIP

Come let us put an end to one thing
   Now that science gives us the power,
And make it impossible for any men
   To exercise for another hour
Any influence on other men that depends
On economic pressure to gain its ends.

Come let us finish the whole damned farce
   Of law and order on murder based,
On the power to coerce and starve and kill,
   With all its hypocrisy, cruelty, and waste;
And safe from all human interference give
Every man at least ample means to live.

Come let us transfer all moral issues
   And social relations to a higher plane
Where men may agree, but if they don't
   Can never be forced to submit again
To the will of others by hunger and want.
It's time to end that sadistic cant.

Come let us put a premium then
   On pure example and persuasive force,
Not that they're likely to carry far
   In maintaining present conventions, of course,
Since these all depend on the belly-grip
And will change completely when that's let slip.

For no religion, no form of government,
   Has ever had any sanction except
Brute needs ruthlessly taken advantage of,
   And these science has now triumphantly o'erleapt.
The fools who say men must still bear any yoke
Have no gifts, save cruelty, more than most other
      folk.

Nor has any other man in politics to-day
  Nor in industry, commerce, or the money swindle,
Nor will any man in the future, thank God.
  Our kings and statesmen in a few years will all
    dwindle
To nothing, big though they may loom to-day,
—Only apprentice nothings upon mankind prey.

There have been men in the course of history
  Giants compared to the mass of their fellows,
But they took no part in the fraud of ruling.
  How big compared to the average, tell us,
Let alone to any the centuries treasure
Are Mosley and Lloyd?—Not a cheese-mite's measure!

Let us believe in the intelligence and decency
  Of the majority of men if properly treated
And their power when a great opportunity
  Is frankly presented to rise and meet it,
And abjure the impious nonentities who still,
As hitherto, would fain impersonate God's will.

All that humanity through the ages has won
  Owes nothing to them or any of their kind,
If our life lost any real asset none
  Of these could attempt to regain it you'd find
—Only a MacDonald, a Baldwin, a Thomas
Are the God-like creatures science threatens to take
    from us!

We'll survive the loss! The kindly common men
  Upstarts like these deem unfit for freedom
Will not have the slightest difficulty
  Once such blind leaders cease to mislead 'em
In establishing a right good fellowship
Forever free of the belly-grip.

THE SEAMLESS GARMENT

Whene'er the mist which stands 'twixt God and thee
Defecates to a pure transparency

Coleridge

You are a cousin of mine
Here in the mill.
It's queer that born in the Langholm
It's no' until
Juist noo I see what it means
To work in the mill like my freen's.

I was tryin' to say something
In a recent poem
Aboot Lenin. You've read a guid lot
In the news—but ken the less o'm?
Look, Wullie, here is his secret noo
In a way I can share it wi' you.

His secret and the secret o' a'
That's worth ocht.
The shuttles fleein' owre quick for my een
Prompt the thocht,
And the coordination atween
Weaver and machine.

The haill shop's dumfoonderin'
To a stranger like me.
Second nature to you; you're perfectly able
To think, speak and see
Apairt frae the looms, tho' to some
That doesna sae easily come.

Lenin was like that wi' workin' class life,
At hame wi't a'.
His fause movements couldna been fewer,
The best weaver Earth ever saw.
A' *he'd* to dae wi' moved intact
Clean, clear, and exact.

fause, false

A poet like Rilke did the same
  In a different sphere,
Made a single reality—a' a'e 'oo'—
  O' his love and pity and fear;
A seamless garment o' music and thought
But you're owre thrang wi' puirer to tak' tent o't.

What's life or God or what you may ca't
  But something at ane like this?
Can you divide yoursel' frae your breath
  Or—if you say yes—
Frae your mind that as in the case
O' the loom keeps that in its place?

Empty vessels mak' the maist noise
  As weel you ken.
Still waters rin deep, owre fu' for soond.
  It's the same wi' men.
Belts fleein', wheels birlin'—a river in flood,
Fu' flow and tension o' poo'er and blood.

Are you equal to life as to the loom?
  Turnin' oot shoddy or what?
Claith better than man? D'ye live to the full,
  Your Poo'er's a' deliverly taught?
Or scamp a'thing else? Border claith's famous.
Shall things o' mair consequence shame us?

Lenin and Rilke baith gied still mair skill,
  Coopers o' Stobo, to a greater concern
Than you devote to claith in the mill.
  Wad it be ill to learn
To keep a bit eye on *their* looms as weel
And no' be hailly ta'en up wi' your 'tweel'?

a' a'e 'oo', all one   thrang, busy   tak' tent o't, take notice of it
ca't, call it   birlin', whirling   claith, cloth   deliverly, continually

The womenfolk ken what I mean.
  Things maun fit like a glove,
Come clean off the spoon—and syne
  There's time for life and love.
The mair we mak' natural as breathin' the mair
Energy for ither things we'll can spare,
  But as lang as we bide like this
Neist to naething we ha'e, or miss.

Want to gang back to the handloom days?
  Nae fear!
Or paintin' oor hides? Hoo d'ye think we've got
  Frae there to here?
We'd get a million times faurer still
If maist folk change profits didna leav't till
A wheen here and there to bring it aboot
—Aye, and hindered no' helped to boot.

Are you helpin'? Machinery's improved, but folk?
  Is't no' high time
We were tryin' to come into line a' roon?
  (I canna think o' a rhyme.)
Machinery in a week mak's greater advances
Than Man's nature twixt Adam and this.

Hundreds to the inch the threids lie in,
  Like the men in a communist cell.
There's a play o' licht frae the factory windas.
  Could you no' mak' mair yoursel'?
Mony a loom mair alive than the weaver seems
For the sun's still nearer than Rilke's dreams.

Ailie Bally's tongue's keepin' time
  To the vibration a' richt.
Clear through the maze your een signal to Jean
  What's for naebody else's sicht
Short skirts, silk stockin's—fegs, hoo the auld
  Emmle-deugs o' the past are curjute and devauld!

wheen, few
emmle-deugs, tatters of clothes   curjute, overthrown
devauld, relinquished

And as for me in my fricative work
  I ken fu' weel
Sic an integrity's what I maun ha'e,
Indivisible, real,
Woven owre close for the point o' a pin
  Onywhere to win in.

34

FIRST HYMN TO LENIN

To Prince D.S. Mirsky

Few even o' the criminals, cravens, and fools
Wha's voices vilify a man they ken
They've cause to fear and are unfit to judge
As they're to stem his influence again
But in the hollows where their herts should be
    Foresee your victory.

Churchills, Locker-Lampsons, Beaverbrooks'll be
In history's perspective less to you
(And them!) than the Centurions to Christ
Of whom, as you, at least this muckle's true
—'Tho' pairtly wrang he cam' to richt amang's
    Faur greater wrangs.'

Christ's cited no' by chance or juist because
You mark the greatest turnin'-point since him
But that your main redress has lain where he's
Least use — fulfillin' his sayin' lang kept dim
That whasae followed him things o' like natur'
    'Ud dae—and greater!

Certes nae ither, if no' you's dune this.
It maitters little. What you've dune's the thing,
No' hoo't compares, corrects, or complements
The work of Christ that's taen owre lang to bring
Sic a successor to keep the reference back
    Natural to mak'.

muckle's much is   **whasae** whoever   **certes** certainly

Great things ha'e aye ta'en great men in the past
In some proportion to the work they did,
But you alane to what you've dune are nocht
Even as the poo'ers to greater ends are hid
In what's ca'd God, or in the common man,
        Withoot your plan.

Descendant o' the unkent Bards wha made
Sang peerless through a' post-anonymous days
I glimpse again in you that mightier poo'er
Than fashes wi' the laurels and the bays
But kens that it is shared by ilka man
        Since time began.

Great things, great men — but at faur greater's cost!
If first things first had had their richtfu' sway
Life and Thocht's misused poo'er might ha' been ane
For a' men's benefit — as still they may
Noo that through you this mair than elemental force
        Has f'und a clearer course.

Christ said: 'Save ye become as bairns again.'
Bairnly eneuch the feck o' us ha' been!
Your work needs men; and its worst foes are juist
The traitors wha through a' history ha' gi'en
The dope that's gar'd the mass o' folk pay heed
        And bide baïrns indeed.

As necessary, and insignificant, as death
Wi' a' its agonies in the cosmos still
The Cheka's horrors are in their degree;
And'll end suner! What maitters 't wha we kill
To lessen that foulest murder that deprives
        Maist men o' real lives?

For now in the flower and iron of the truth
To you we turn; and turn in vain nae mair,
Ilka fool has folly eneuch for sadness
But at last we are wise and wi' laughter tear
The veil of being, and are face to face
        Wi' the human race.

fashes, bothers **feck, majority** **bide, remain**

Here lies your secret, O Lenin, — yours and oors,
No' in the majority will that accepts the result
But in the real will that bides its time and kens
The benmaist resolve is the poo'er in which we exult
Since naebody's willingly deprived o' the good;
And, least o' a', the crood!

35

SECOND HYMN TO LENIN

Ah, Lenin, you were richt. But I'm a poet
(And you c'ud mak allowances for that!)
Aimin' at mair than you aimed at
Tho' yours comes first, I know it.

An unexamined life is no' worth ha'in'.
Yet Burke was richt; owre muckle concern
Wi' Life's foundations is a sure
Sign o' decay; tho' Joyce in turn

Is richt, and the principal question
Aboot a work o' art is frae hoo deep
A life it springs—and syne hoo faur
Up frae't it has the poo'er to leap.

And hoo muckle it lifts up wi' it
Into the sunlicht like a saumon there,
Universal Spring! For Morand's richt—
It s'ud be like licht in the air—

Are my poems spoken in the factories and fields,
In the streets o' the toon?
Gin they're no, then I'm failin' to dae
What I ocht to ha' dune.

ha'in', having

Gin I canna win through to the man in the street,
The wife by the hearth,
A' the cleverness on earth 'll no' mak' up
For the damnable dearth.

Haud on, haud on; what poet's dune that?
Is Shakespeare read,
Or Dante or Milton or Goethe or Burns?
—You heard what I said.

—A means o' world locomotion,
The maist perfected and aerial o' a'.
Lenin's name's gane owre the haill earth,
But the names o' the ithers?—Ha!

What hidie-hole o' the vineyard d'they scart
Wi' minds like the look on a hen's face,
Morand, Joyce, Burke, and the rest
That e'er wrote; me noo in like case?

Great poets hardly onybody kens o'?
Geniuses like a man talkin' t'm sel'?
Nonsense! They're nocht o' the sort
Their character's easy to tell.

They're nocht but romantic rebels
Strikin' dilettante poses;
Trotsky—Christ, no' wi' a croon o' thorns
But a wreath o' paper roses.

A' that's great is free and expansive.
What ha' they expanded tae?
They've affected nocht but a fringe
O' mankind in ony way.

Barbarian saviour o' civilization
Hoo weel ye kent (we're owre dull witted)
Naething is dune save as we ha'e
Means to en's transparently fitted.

scart, scratch at t'm sel', to himself

Poetry like politics maun cut
The cackle and pursue real ends,
Unerringly as Lenin, and to that
Its nature better tends.

Wi' Lenin's vision equal poet's gift
And what unparalleled force was there!
Nocht in a' literature wi' that
Begins to compare.

Nae simple rhymes for silly folk
But the haill art, as Lenin gied
Nae Marx-without tears to workin' men
But the fu' course insteed.

Organic constructional work,
Practicality, and work by degrees;
First things first; and poetry in turn
'Ll be built by these.

You saw it faur off when you thocht
O' mass-education yet.
Hoo lang till they rise to Pushkin?
And that's but a fit!

Oh, it's nonsense, nonsense, nonsense,
Nonsense at this time o' day
That breid-and-butter problems
S'ud be in ony man's way.

They s'ud be like the tails we tint
On leavin' the monkey stage;
A' maist folk fash aboot's alike
Primaeval to oor age.

We're grown ups that haena yet
Put bairnly things aside
—A' that's material and moral—
And oor new state descried.

fit, foot   tint, lost   fash, bother   bairnly, childish

Sport, love, and parentage,
Trade, politics, and law
S'ud be nae mair to us than braith
We hardly ken we draw.

Freein' oor poo'ers for greater things,
And fegs there's plenty o' them,
Tho' wha's still trammelt in alow
Canna be tenty o' them—

In the meantime Montéhus' sangs—
But as you were ready to tine
The Russian Revolution to the German
Gin that ser'd better syne,

Or foresaw that Russia maun lead
The workers' cause, and then
Pass the lead elsewhere, and aiblins
Fa' faur backward again,

Sae here, twixt poetry and politics,
There's nae doot in the en'.
Poetry includes that and s'ud be
The greatest poo'er amang men.

—It's the greatest, *in posse* at least,
That men ha'e discovered yet
Tho' nae doot they're unconscious still
O' ithers faur greater than it.

You confined yoursel' to your work
—A step at a time;
But, as the loon is in the man,
That'll be ta'en up i' the rhyme,

Ta'en up like a pool in the sands
Aince the tide rows in,
When life opens its hert and sings
Withoot scruple or sin.

fegs, faith   alow, below   tenty, mindful   tine, lose
aiblins, perhaps   loon, boy   rows, rolls

Your knowledge in your ain sphere
Was exact and complete
But your sphere's elementary and sune by
As a poet maun see't.

For a poet maun see in a' thing,
Ev'n what looks trumpery or horrid,
A subject equal to ony
—A star for the forehead!

A poet has nae choice left
Betwixt Beaverbrook, say, and God.
Jimmy Thomas or you,
A cat, carnation, or clod.

He daurna turn awa' frae ocht
For a single act o' neglect
And straucht he may fa' frae grace
And be void o' effect.

Disinterestedness,
Oor profoundest word yet,
But how far yont even that
The sense o' onything's set!

The inward necessity yont
Ony laws o' cause
The intellect conceives
That a'thing has!

Freend, foe; past, present, future;
Success, failure; joy, fear;
Life, Death; and a'thing else,
For us, are equal here.

Male, female; quick or deid,
Let us fike nae mair;
The deep line o' cleavage
Disna lie there.

sune by, soon past **daurna, dare not**
straucht, immediately **fike, trouble**

Black in the pit the miner is,
The shepherd reid on the hill,
And I'm wi' them baith until
The end of mankind, I wis.

Whatever their jobs a' men are ane
In life, and syne in daith
(Tho' it's sma' patience I can ha'e
Wi' life's ideas o' that by the way)
And he's nae poet but kens it, faith,
And ony job but the hardest's ta'en.

The sailor gangs owre the curve o' the sea,
The housewife's thrang in the wash-tub,
And whatna rhyme can I find but hub
And what else can poetry be?

The core o' a' activity,
Changin't in accordance wi'
Its inward necessity
And mede o' integrity.

Unremittin', relentless,
Organized to the last degree,
Ah Lenin, politics is bairns' play
To what this maun be!

wis, know

36

THIRD HYMN TO LENIN

for Muriel Rukeyser

None can usurp this height (returned that shade)
But those to whom the miseries of the world
Are miseries, and will not let them rest. Keats, *Hyperion*

These that have turned the world upside down are come hither also. Acts *xvii*, 6

The night is far spent, the day is at hand, let us therefore cast off the works of darkness, and let us put on the armour of light. Romans *xiii*, 12

Glasgow is a city of the sea, but what avails
In this great human Sargasso even that flair,
That resolution to understand all bearings
That is the essence of a seaman's character,
The fruit of first-hand education in the ways of ships,
The ways of man, and the ways of women even more,
Since these resemble sea and weather most
And are the deepest source of all appropriate lore.

A cloud no bigger than a man's hand, a new
Note in the wind, an allusion over the salt-junk,
And seamen are aware of 'a number of things'.
That sense of concealed but powerful meanings sunk
In hints that almost pass too quick to seize,
Which must be won out of the abysses
Above and below, is second nature to them
But not enough in such a sink as this is.

What seaman in the history of the world before
On such an ocean as you sailed could say
This wave will recede, this advance, knew every wave
By name, and foresaw its inevitable way
And the final disposition of the whirling whole;
So identified at every point with the historic flow
That, even as you pronounced, so it occurred?
You turned a whole world right side up, and did so
With no dramatic gesture, no memorable word.
Now measure Glasgow for a like laconic overthrow!

On days of revolutionary turning points you literally
flourished,
Became clairvoyant, foresaw the movement of classes,
And the probable zig-zags of the revolution
As if on your palm;
Not only an analytical mind but also
A great constructive, synthesizing mind
Able to build up in thought the new reality
As it must actually come
By force of definite laws eventually,
Taking into consideration, of course,
Conscious interference, the bitter struggle
For the tasks still before the Party, and the class it leads
As well as possible diversions and inevitable actions
Of all other classes.—Such clairvoyance is the result
Of a profound and all-sided knowledge of life
With all its richness of colour, connexions and relations.
Hence the logic of your speeches — 'like some all-powerful
feelers
Economic, political, ideological, and so forth.
Which grasp, once for all, all sides as in a vise,
And one has no strength left to tear away from their
embrace;
Either one yields or decides upon complete failure.'

As some great seaman or some poet grasps
The practical meaning, ideal beauty, traditional fascination,
Intellectual importance and emotional chances combined
In any instant in his particular situation,
So here there is a like accumulation of effects,
On countless planes of significance at once,
And all we see is set in riddling terms,
Making aught but myriad-mindedness a dunce.

How can the points be taken quickly enough,
Meaning behind meaning, dense forests of cross-reference;
How can the wood be seen for such a chaos of trees;
How from the hydra's mouths glean any sense?
The logic and transitions of the moment taken,
On the spur of the moment all the sheer surface
And rapid narrative 'the public wants' secured,
How grasp the 'darker purposes' and win controlling
place?

We are but fools who live by headlines else,
Surfriders merely of the day's sensations,
Living in the flicker like a cinema fan,
Nor much dedoped, defooled, by any patience.
Mere Study's fingers cannot grasp the roots of power.
Be with me, Lenin, reincarnate in me here,
Fathom and solve as you did Russia erst
This lesser maze, you greatest proletarian seer!

Hard test, my master, for another reason.
The whole of Russia had no Hell like this.*
There is no place in all the white man's world
So sunk in the unspeakable abyss.
Only a country whose chief glory is the Kirk,
A country with our fetish of efficiency and thrift,
With endless loving sentiment to mask the facts,
Has such an infernal masterpiece in its gift.

A horror that might sicken your stomach even,
The peak of the capitalist system and the trough of Hell,
Fit testimonial to our ultra-pious race,
A people greedy, lying, and unconscionable
Beyond compare.—Seize on this link, spirit of Lenin, then
And you must needs haul upwards to the light
The whole base chain of the phenomena that hold
Europe so far below levels worthy of its might!

Do you know the haunting slum smell? Do you remember
Proust's account of a urinal's dark-green and yellow scent,
Or Gillies' remark when Abelard complained
Of Guibert's horrible cooking, worse than excrement,
Yet he had watched him scour the crocks himself:
'He never washes the cloth he scrubs them with.
That gives the taste, the odour; the world's worst yet.'
But no! We've progressed. Words fail for this all-
pervasive
Slum stench. A corpse beside it is a violet.

* i.e. the slums of Glasgow.

Door after door as we knocked was opened by a shirted man, suddenly and softly as if impelled forward by the overpowering smell behind him. It is this smell which is the most oppressive symbol of such lives; choking, nauseating; the smell of corrupt sweat and unnamed filthiness of body. That smell! Sometimes it crept out at us past the legs of the householder, insinuatingly, as if ashamed; sometimes it brazened out foul and pestiferous. Once in a woman's shilling boarding-house it leapt out and took us by the throat like an evil beast. The smell of the slums, the unforgettable, the abominable smell!
Bolitho: *The Cancer of Empire*, describing the slums of Glasgow.

Ah, lizard eyes, how I would love to see
You reincarnate here and taking issue
With the piffling spirits of our public men,
Going through them like a machine-gun through crinkled
tissue,
But first of all — in Cranston's tea-rooms* say —
With some of our leading wart-hogs calmly sat
Watching the creatures' sardonically toothsome faces
Die out in horror like Alice's Cheshire cat.

We, who have seen the daemons one by one
Emerging in the modern world and know full well
Our rapport with the physical world is safe
So long as we avoid all else and dwell,
Heedless of the multiplicity of correspondences
Behind them, on the simple data our normal senses give,
Know what vast liberating powers these dark powers
disengage,
But leave the task to others and in craven safety live.

Normal, thanks to the determined blindness we possess
To all that might upset our little apple-carts,
Too cautious to do anything about it,
Knowing our days are brief, though these slum parts
Harbour hosts of larves, legions of octopuses,
Pulsing in the dark air, with the wills and powers
To rise in scaly depravity to unthinkable heights
And annihilate forever all that is ours.

* Well-known Glasgow restaurant, former resort of Glasgow Labour MPs and leading supporters.

And only here and there a freak like me
Looking at himself, all of him, with intensest scrutiny,
See how he runs round like a dog, every particle
Concentrated on getting in safe somewhere, while he
With equal determination must push himself out,
Feel more at all costs, experience more, be shattered more,
Driven towards an unqualifiable upward and onward
That is — all morons feel — suicidally over the score.

Our frantic efforts go all ways and go none;
Incontinent with vain hopes, tireless Micawbers,
Banking on what Gladstone said in 1890
Or Christ a few centuries earlier, — there's
No lack of counsellors, of *die List der Vernunft.*
The way to Hell is paved with plenty of talk,
But nothing ever happens — nothing ever will;
The future's always rosy, the present no less black.

Clever — and yet we cannot solve this problem even;
Civilised — and flaunting such a monstrous sore;
Christian — in flat defiance of all Christ taught;
Proud of our country with this open sewer at our door,
Come, let us shed all this transparent bluff,
Acknowledge our impotence, the prize eunuchs of Europe,
Battening on our shame, and with voices weak as bats'
Proclaiming in ghoulish kirks our base immortal hope.

And what is this impossible problem then?
Only to give a few thousand people enough to eat,
Decent houses and a fair income every week.
What? For nothing? Yes! Scotland can well afford it.

It cannot be done. The poor are always with us,
The Bible says. Would other countries agree?
Clearly we couldn't unless they did it too.
All the old arguments against ending Slavery!

Ah, no! These bourgeois hopes are not our aim.

Lenin, lover of music, who dare not listen to it,
Teach us to eschew all the siren voices too
And get due *Diesseitigkeit.* Countless petty indulgences
—We give them fine names, like Culture, it is true—
Lure us up this enchanting side-line and up that
When we should stay in stinking vennel and wynd,
Not masturbating our immortal souls,
But simply doing some honest service to mankind.

Great forces dedicated to the foulest ends
Are reaping a rich victory in Glasgow here
In life stunted and denied and endless misery,
Preventible disease and 'crime' and death; and standing sheer
Behind these crowded thoroughfares with armaments concealed
Ready at any vital move to massacre
These mindless mobs, the gangsters lurk, the officer class,
    ruthless
Watching Glasgow's every step and lusting to attack her.

And freedom's opposing forces are hidden too,
But Fascism has its secret agents everywhere
In every coward's castle, shop, bank, manse and school
While few serve Freedom's counter-service there,
Nor can they serve — for all but all men's ears
Are deaf to aught it says, stuffed with the wax
Of ignorant prejudice and subsidised inanity
Till Freedom to their minds all access lacks.

And most insidious and stultifying of all
The anti-human forces have instilled the thought
That knowledge has outrun the individual brain
Till trifling details only can be brought
Within the scope of any man; and so have turned
Humanity's vast achievements against the human mind
Until a sense of general impotence compels
Most men in petty grooves to stay confined.

This is the lie of lies — the High Treason to mankind.
No one but fritters half his time away.
It is the human instinct — the will to use it — that's destroyed
Till only one or two in every million men today
Know that thought is reality—and thought alone!—
And must absorb all the material — their goal
The mastery by the spirit of all the facts that can be known.

Instead of that we have a Jeans accommodating the stars
To traditional superstitions, and a Barnes who thrids
Divers geometries — Euclidean, Lobatchewskyan,
Riemannian —
And Cepheid variables, white dwarfs, yet stubbornly
heads
(Though he admits his futile journey fails to reach
Any solution of the problem of 'God's' relation to Time)
Back to his starting place — to a like betrayal
Of the scientific spirit to a dud Sublime.

And in Scotland a Haldane even, rendering great service
to biological theory
In persistently calling attention to the special form of
organization
Existing in living things — yet failing greatly
Through his defeatist wish to accept
This principle of organization as axiomatic
Instead of tracing its relation to the lower principle of
organization
Seen in paracrystals, colloids, and so forth.
Threading with great skill the intricate shuttling path
From 'spontaneity' to preoccupation with design,
From the realistic 'moment' to the abstraction of essential
form
And ending with a fusion of all their elements,
At once realistic and abstract.

> *Daring and unblushing atheism is creeping abroad and saturating the working population, which are the proper persons to be saturated with it. I look to no others. It has been said to me by more than one person, 'Let us write in the style of Hume and Gibbon and seek readers among the higher classes.' I answer 'No', I know nothing of the so-called higher classes but that they are robbers; I will work towards the raising of the working population above them.* — Richard Carlile

Or like Michael Roberts whose *New Country*
Is the same old country, and mediaeval enough his
'modern mind'
Confessing that after all he cannot see
How civilization can be saved unless confined
Under the authority of a Church which in the West
Can only be the so-called Christian Church.
Perish the thought! Let us take our stand
Not on this infernal old parrot's perch
But squarely with Richard Carlile: 'The enemy with
whom we have to grapple
Is one with whom no peace can be made. Idolatry will not
parley,
Superstition will not treat or covenant. They must be
uprooted
Completely for public and individual safety.'

Michael Roberts and All Angels! Auden, Spender, those
bhoyos,
All yellow twicers: not one of them
With a tithe of Carlile's courage and integrity.
Unlike these pseudos I am *of* — not *for* — the working class
And like Carlile know nothing of the so-called higher
classes
Save only that they are cheats and murderers,
Battening like vampires on the masses.

The illiteracy of the literate! But Glasgow's hordes
Are not even literate save a man or two;
All bogged in words that communicate no thought,
Only mumbo-jumbo, fraudulent clap-trap, ballyhoo.
The idiom of which constructive thought avails itself
Is unintelligible save to a small minority
And all the rest wallow in exploded fallacies
And cherish for immortal souls their gross stupidity,
While in the deeper layers of their ignorance who delves
Finds in this order — Scotland, other men, themselves.
We do not play or keep any mere game's conventions.
Our concern is human wholeness — the child-like spirit
Newborn every day — not, indeed, as careless of tradition
Nor of the lessons of the past: these it must needs inherit.

But as capable of such complete assimilation and surrender,
So all-inclusive, unfenced-off, uncategoried, sensitive and tender.
The growth is unconditioned and unwarped — Ah, Lenin,
Life and that more abundantly, thou Fire of Freedom,
Fire-like in your purity and heaven-seeking vehemence,
Yet the adjective must not suggest merely meteoric,
Spectacular — not the flying sparks but the intense
Glowing core of your character, your large and splendid stability
Made you the man you were — the live heart of all humanity!

Spirit of Lenin, light on this city now!

Light up this city now!

37

REFLECTIONS IN A SLUM

A lot of the old folk here—all that's left
Of them after a lifetime's infernal thrall
Remind me of a Bolshie the 'whites' buried alive
Up to his nose, just able to breathe, that's all.

Watch them. You'll see what I mean. When found
His eyes had lost their former gay twinkle.
Ants had eaten *that* away; but there was still
Some life in him . . . his forehead *would* wrinkle!

And I remember Gide telling
Of Valéry and himself:
'It was a long time ago. We were young.
We had mingled with idlers
Who formed a circle
Round a troupe of wretched mountebanks.
It was on a raised strip of pavement
In the boulevard Saint Germain,
In front of the Statue of Broca.
They were admiring a poor woman,

Thin and gaunt, in pink tights, despite the cold.
Her team-mate had tied her, trussed her up,
Skilfully from head to foot,
With a rope that went round her
I don't know how many times,
And from which, by a sort of wriggling,
She was to manage to free herself.
Sorry image of the fate of the masses!
But no one thought of the symbol.
The audience merely contemplated
In stupid bliss the patient's efforts.
She twisted, she writhed, slowly freed one arm,
Then the other, and when at last
The final cord fell from her
Valéry took me by the arm:
"Let's go now! She has ceased suffering!"'

Oh, if only ceasing to suffer
They were able to become men.
Alas! how many owe their dignity,
Their claim on our sympathy,
Merely to their misfortune.
Likewise, so long as a plant has not blossomed
One can hope that its flowering will be beautiful.
What a mirage surrounds what has not yet blossomed!
What a disappointment when one can no longer
Blame the abjection on the deficiency!
It is good that the voice of the indigent,
Too long stifled, should manage
To make itself heard.
But I cannot consent to listen
To nothing but that voice.
Man does not cease to interest me
When he ceases to be miserable.
Quite the contrary!
That it is important to aid him
In the beginning goes without saying,
Like a plant it is essential
To water at first,
But this is in order to get it to flower
And I *am concerned with the blossom.*

38

KRASSIVY

Scotland has had few men whose names
Matter—or should matter—to intelligent people,
But of these Maclean, next to Burns, was the greatest
And it should be of him, with every Scotsman and Scotswoman
To the end of time, as it was of Lenin in Russia
When you might talk to a woman who had been
A young girl in 1917 and find
That the name of Stalin lit no fires,
But when you asked her if she had seen Lenin
Her eyes lighted up and her reply
Was the Russian word which means
Both beautiful and red,
Lenin, she said, was '*krassivy, krassivy*'.
John Maclean too was '*krassivy, krassivy*',
A description no other Scot has ever deserved.

39

JOHN MACLEAN (1879–1923)

All the buildings in Glasgow are grey
With cruelty and meanness of spirit,
But once in a while one greyer than the rest
    A song shall merit
Since a miracle of true courage is seen
For a moment its walls between.

Look at it, you fools, with unseeing eyes
And deny it with lying lips!
But your craven bowels well know what it is
    And hasten to eclipse
In a cell, as black as the shut boards of the Book
You lie by, the light no coward can brook.

It is not the blue of heaven that colours
The blue jowls of your thugs of police,
And 'justice' may well do its filthy work
Behind walls as filthy as these
And congratulate itself blindly and never know
The prisoner takes the light with him as he goes below.

Stand close, stand close, and block out the light
As long as you can, you ministers and lawyers,
Hulking brutes of police, fat bourgeoisie,
Sleek derma for congested guts—its fires
Will leap through yet; already it is clear
Of all MacLean's foes not one was his peer.

As Pilate and the Roman soldiers to Christ
Were Law and Order to the finest Scot of his day,
One of the few true men in our sordid breed,
A flash of sun in a country all prison-grey.
Speak to others of Christian charity; I cry again
For vengeance on the murderers of John MacLean.
Let the light of truth in on the base pretence
Of Justice that sentenced him behind these grey walls.
All law is the contemptible fraud he declared it.
Like a lightning-bolt at last the workers' wrath falls
On all such castles of cowards whether they be
Uniformed in ermine, or blue, or khaki.

Royal honours for murderers and fools! The 'fount of honour'
Is poisoned and spreads its corruption all through,
But Scotland will think yet of the broken body
And unbreakable spirit, MacLean, of you,
And know you were indeed the true tower of its strength,
As your prison of its foul stupidity, at length.

40

GLASGOW 1960*

Returning to Glasgow after long exile
Nothing seemed to me to have changed its style.
Buses and trams all labelled 'To Ibrox'
Swung past packed tight as they'd hold with folks.
Football match, I concluded, but just to make sure
I asked; and the man looked at me fell dour,
Then said, 'Where in God's name are *you* frae, sir?
It'll be a record gate, but the cause o' the stir
Is a debate on "la loi de l'effort converti"
Between Professor MacFadyen and a Spainish pairty.'
I gasped. The newsboys came running along,
'Special! Turkish Poet's Abstruse New Song.
Scottish Authors' Opinions'—and, holy snakes,
I saw the edition sell like hot cakes.

41

THE DEAD LIEBKNECHT
(After the German of Rudolf Leonhardt)

His corpse owre a' the city lies
In ilka square and ilka street.
His spilt bluid floods the vera skies
And nae hoose but is darkened wi't.

The factory horns begin to blaw
Thro' a' the city, blare on blare,
The lowsin' time o' workers a',
Like emmits skailin' everywhere.

And wi' his white teeth shinin' yet
The corpse lies smilin' underfit.

* Written some years earlier than 1960.
lowsin', unyoking emmits, ants
skailin', pouring out

42

AT THE CENOTAPH

Are the living so much use
That we need to mourn the dead?
Or would it yield better results
To reverse their roles instead?
The millions slain in the War—
Untimely, the best of our seed?—
Would the world be any the better
If they were still living indeed?
The achievements of such as are
To the notion lend no support;
The whole history of life and death
Yields no scrap of evidence for't.—
Keep going to your wars, you fools, as of yore;
I'm the civilisation you're fighting for.

43

PRAYER FOR A SECOND FLOOD

There'd ha'e to be nae warnin'. Times ha'e changed
And Noahs are owre numerous nooadays,
(And them the vera folk to benefit maist!)
Knock the feet frae under them, O Lord, wha praise
Your unsearchable ways sae muckle and yet hope
    To keep within knowledgeable scope!

Ding a' their trumpery show to blauds again.
Their measure is the thimblefu' o' Esk in spate.
Like whisky the tittlin' craturs mete oot your poo'ers
Aince a week for bawbees in the kirk-door plate,
—And pit their umbrellas up when they come oot
    If mair than a pulpitfu' o' You's aboot!

muckle, much   ding, smash   blauds, pieces
tittlin', whispering   bawbees, ha'pennies

O arselins wi' them! Whummle them again!
Coup them heels-owre-gowdy in a storm sae gundy
That mony a lang fog-theekit face I ken
'll be sooked richt doon under through a cundy
In the High Street, afore you get weel-sterted
    And are still hauf-herted!

Then flush the world in earnest. Let yoursel' gang,
Scour't to the bones, and mak' its marrow holes
Toom as a whistle as they used to be
In days I mind o' ere men fidged wi' souls,
But naething had forgotten you as yet,
    Nor you forgotten it.

Up then and at them, ye Gairds o' Heaven,
The Divine Retreat is owre. Like a tidal bore
Boil in among them; let the lang lugs nourished
On the milk o' the word at last hear the roar
O' human shingle; and replenish the salt o' the earth
    In the place o' their birth.

44

FROM AN 'ODE TO ALL REBELS'

'*Deluded men despise me when I have taken human form.*'
Bhagavad-Gita, *ix*, II. Cf. John *i*, 10

As the heavy earth is the same below
Though insubstantialised in the sunshine
I see a man's slack mouth and goggling eyes
Behind this glory and know them for mine
Nor if I could would I lose for a moment
Divine in human or human in divine.
O double vision fighting in the glass!
Now light blots out this last distinction of class.

arselins, on their arse   whummle, tumble   coup, upend
heels-owre-gowdy, head over heels   gundy, ravenous
fog-theekit, moss-thatched   cundy, conduit   Toom, clean
fidged, itched   lugs, ears

O magical change, O miracle
I am suddenly beyond myself.
  Red, white, and square,
Tearing the soul to rags!

Folk recognise—with regret it may be—
Man's kinship with the most loathsome brute
Joggling his protruding sternum there
And letting his animal noises out,
    All they can have patience with,
    All they can pity,
All they can hide in their madhouses,
    In their gaols and hospital wards,
All that's diseased, misshapen, obscene,
    Mankind accepts and guards;
But when an angel appears, a man
Infinitely superior to man, as here,
From a man no better than other men,
An idiot like them, they howl with fear,
Or perjure their sight, and gibe and jeer
And deny that the like can ever appear,
    Let alone be one with the other.

'L'extrême esprit est accusé de folie
  Comme l'extrême défaut.
Rien que la médiocrité est bon.
  C'est sortir de l'humanité
  Que de sortir du milieu.'

'Und wir, die an steigendes Glück
denken, empfanden die Rührung,
die uns beinah bestürzt,
wenn ein Glückliches fällt.'

It's against all sense and what's the use
Of decency, worship, a shepherded soul,
If a creature like this can suddenly emerge—
Regardless of all most men can thole,
Yet visibly dowered with the light of lights,
The glory of God he shows yet denies,
When even if they tried like vices themselves,
Instead of the wisdom and virtues they prize,
None of them, not even the most reverend and upright,
Would ever be transfigured in similar wise?

God should consult with the Government or Church
Or get the medical profession to advise,
Not act in such an irrational way
In deciding on who He glorifies,
And not—as too often—let scallywags,
Lechers and topers, win such a prize.
With due respect we'll not follow His lead.
Mankind at least must always keep its head.
The wise are confounded, calculations upset,
Law set at naught, and order contemned—
O the Angel of Death is covered with eyes
But I stand in a guise still more terribly gemmed.—
    I think you are right.
    Culture's leading to the extinction of Man.
    What? Stop the culture?
      That's not my plan.

I am Ishmael, the only man
Who's the friend of all men
(And who has ever known certitude
Must here recognise its voice again!)
    I tell you all else is vain.

—Every man who havers about honest toil
And believes in rewards and punishments,
In a God like Public Opinion
Or conformable to human reason,
And the sanctity of the financial system,
All that appeal to the Past or the Future,
Or think that two and two made four,
Or that they can judge 'twixt virtue and vice,
Health and disease, sanity and insanity,
Or that thought can be its own judge;
Who cannot believe in something for nothing
(Not stopping to ask whence their very lives come);
Every man who is afraid of leisure,
Every man who with needless toil shuts out
The free, abundant, intolerable light;
All the men of science, the enemies of truth;
All imposers and accepters of any taboos;
All taskmasters and their bondagers,
Every man who says we must hold together.
Dependent on each other—not just on God;
That we are members of one another

And cannot stand alone—not wholly alone—
Or escape from the old apron-strings and cry
'Woman, what have you to do with me?'
All who are afraid of becoming too clever
And prefer a decent stupidity;
All who cry: 'Hold—that's going too far.
We don't know where—if at all—it'll stop;'
All who believe we should be of one mind
Or at least agreed upon certain things,
Obey the same laws, honour the same God,
Subscribe to some 'common humanity';
Deny that the wind always blows when it lists
And isn't in the habit of answering prayer;
Say that God prefers the just to the unjust,
That differences are only evolved to be
Resumed into undifferentiated oneness again;
All who trust any external authority,
All short circuiters of consciousness,
Believers in any State or system or creed,
All who expect clear explanations,
Fixed standards, and reasonable methods,
All the rulers and all the ruled,
        And everybody else,
These are the devils, the impious ideas;
Rebels, all cries of 'Hold—have a care!'
        Tell us where our enemies are.
Our task is to destroy them all and return
Victorious to the spirit that in us should burn,
Our sole concern, that all but all men spurn,
And that spurns all men—all men, even us;
And can make nothing of the word victorious.

45

THINK NOT THAT I FORGET

Think not that I forget a single pang
Of all that folk have tholed.
Agonies and abominations beyond all telling.
Sights to daunt the most bold.

There are buildings in every town where daily
Unthinkable horrors take place,
I am the woman in cancer's toils,
The man without a face.

I am all cruelty and lust and filth,
Corruption and law-made crime—
The helpless prisoners badgered in their cells
In every land and clime,

All 'gallant soldiers' murdering for pay
(Plus 'little Belgium' or like affair)
And heroic airmen blithe to give
Poor tribes Death from the air,

And all the hidden but no less hideous deeds
Sound citizens are always privily at—
Only in the mean natures and vicious looks
Of their children, themselves, or their underlings caught.

Oh, there's as much of it in Great Britain here
As in Sing Sing or in Cayenne
Differently disguised of course and hiding
In the most decent and God-fearing men.

There is no horror history's ever known
Mob passion or greedy fear wouldn't soon
Make them do over again—slovens and cowards
Moving pig-eyed in their daily round.

They face nothing—their whole lives depend
On ignorance and base contempt
For all that's worth-while in the powers of Man
From any share in it exempt.

In the midst of plenty in poverty,—
To Art no better than apes—
Think not that I am unaware
Of one of their loathsome shapes.

Aristocratic sentiments?—Yes! But remember
These Yahoos belong to no single class.
You'll find far more in proportion to numbers
In palaces and west-end clubs than in the mass.

46

LIGHT AND SHADOW

Like memories of what cannot be
Within the reign of memory . . .
That shake our mortal frames to dust.
Shelley

On every thought I have the countless shadows fall
Of other thoughts as valid that I cannot have;
Cross-lights of errors, too, impossible to me,
Yet somehow truer than all these thoughts, being with
more power aglow.

May I never lose these shadowy glimpses of unknown thoughts
That modify and minify my own, and never fail
To keep some shining sense of the way all thoughts at last
Before life's dawning meaning like the stars at sunrise pale.

47

ON THE OCEAN FLOOR

Now more and more on my concern with the lifted
waves of genius gaining
I am aware of the lightless depths that beneath them lie;
And as one who hears their tiny shells incessantly raining
On the ocean floor as the foraminifera die.

48

O EASE MY SPIRIT

And as for their appearances they had one likeness as if a wheel had been in the midst of a wheel.

Ezekiel

O ease my spirit increasingly of the load
Of my personal limitations and the riddling differences
Between man and man with a more constant insight
Into the fundamental similarity of all activities.

And quicken me to the gloriously and terribly illuminating
Integration of the physical and the spiritual till I feel how easily
I could put my hand gently on the whole round world
As on my sweetheart's head and draw it to me.

49

AGAINST INFANTILISM

Art must be related to the central issues of life,
Not serve a sub-artistic purpose that could as well
Be served by the possession of a new motor-car
Or a holiday on the Continent perhaps.
What do we Scottish writers most lack, most need?
—An immediate experience of the concrete,
A rich overflowing apprehension of the definite
Day-by-day content of our people's lives,
A burningly clear understanding of the factors at work,
Of the actual correlation of the forces, in labour to-day;
A Dundee jute mill, Singer's, Beardmore's,
The ghost towns, ruined fishing villages, slave camps,
And all the derelict areas of our countryside;
The writer not first and foremost concerned with these
Lacks the centrality that alone can give
Value to his work—he is a trifler, a traitor,
To his art and to mankind alike,
A fool choosing flight and fantasy,
Not to be pitied, but despised.

It is a lying cry to say
That human nature cannot be changed.
It can be, and is being, completely.
We are long past the time when doubt of an accepted system
Liberates great minds while yet the system itself
Has not fallen into such contempt as to be
Incapable of their action within its limits.
Long past the affectation of being above the battle,
Of being socially agnostic, seeing all systems
As subject to historic change, and the will
Of great men, and accepting none.

Yet what are all our intellectuals saying?
All victimized by repetition-compulsion
They are denying these huge horizons opening out
And crying 'Fundamentally man cannot change'
And bleating 'After all there's but one kind of man.
Men's ways of thought can never become
So inconceivably different from ours!'
Can't they? They have already. Mine have
And every fit member's of the I.U.R.W.
And are speedily disposing of the bourgeois notions
That art must be 'neutral, equally indifferent
To good and evil, knowing no pity, no anger'.
And that 'neither in its high countenance
Nor looks can its secret thoughts be read',
Any more than the masked wizard-of-History's can.
We have read them all right!
The overcoming by life of its own limitations
The calling out of the major images of the future,
What and as is—and as should and will be
Reality in motion, advancing and developing
Not for us? They can keep their decrepit
Terms, which belong to a past we've sloughed off
Of realism, romanticism, classicism,
Naturalism, and all the witless rest
Of isms, flourishing in the parent mire of scholasticism.

(The primary capitalistic neurosis is narcissism.)
It is a libel to say we need these infantilisms now
And always will—lest these precious little scribblers
Prove Rip Van Winkles on the edge of by far
The greatest Kulturkampf in human history,
These fools who have already become unreadable
Not because their actual craftsmanship has degenerated,
But simply because, in the most literal sense,
They do not know what they are talking about.
So with our Scottish writers; they are forced
Either to distort the content of Scottish life
In order to make it conform
To some desperate personal wish-fulfilment
Or flee from it entirely—into the past,
Into fantasy, or some other reality-surrogate.
Outside the revolutionary movement there is no place
For any writer worth a moment's thought.
The 'culture class' for which they think they write
Has ceased to exist either as a class
Or as a repository of culture; as the strain
Of economic struggle tightens the so-called
Middle-class vanguard immediately reveals
Its essential moral weakness and above all
Its intellectual poverty thinly coated
By a veneer of artistic sophistication;
No self-respecting man can have anything to say to them.
They have no longer any real reason for existing,
And therefore literature and art can be nothing
For them except day-dreams or 'shots' in the arm,
While a few of them, the sentimental stoics,
May read such a poem as this (or bits of it)
With a wearily-approving nod of cynicism.

There is nothing whatever in contemporary biology
Either the science of heredity or of genetics,
Nothing we know of the mechanisms of inheritance,
Nothing in the nature of the genes or chromosomes
To stand in the way of the radicals' enthusiasm
For social transformation—the revolutionists'
Advocacy of profoundly-altered social systems.
On the other hand there is a vast accumulation
Of evidence from the sociological sciences,
Economy, anthropology, sociology,
Politics, the philosophy of history, to substantiate

The necessity, the sanity, and the wisdom
Of deep changes in all institutions, customs,
Habits, values—in short, civilizations.
Human nature is the last thing we need to worry about.
Let us attend to the circumstances that condition it.

We live in a world that has become
Intolerable as the subject of passive reflection.
What is our response to the unescapable reality?
Are we too like these miserable little cliques to turn
Because of theoretic inadequacy
From social causation, from the poetry of purgative action
And try to find form and significance
In pure feeling itself, transplanted and re-imagined,
Seeking the meaning of experience in the phenomena of
   experience,
Pure sensation becoming an ultimate value
In the neurotic and mystical attempt
To give physicality an intellectual content,
In the sensitizing of nerves already raw,
Meaningless emotion aroused automatically
Without satisfaction or education, as in melodrama,
Man can find his own dignity only in action now.

Scottish writers, the height and depth of your writings
Will be measured by the extent to which
The dialectics of our era find expression
In the artistic imagery—how widely, forcefully, clearly
(Sir Thomas Inskip permitting or not!)
The burning contemporary problems are expressed in it,
The class war, the struggles and ideals
Of the proletariat bent on changing the world,
And consequently on changing human nature.

50

AN ENGLISH WAR-POET

This poem, while not included in The Battle Continues, *his Spanish War poem, published by the Castle Wynd Printers Ltd, was written at the same time and deals with the English reaction to Spain and to war in general.*

In another respect the Spanish War
—Fought on the Republican side
Not by doped conscripts, foreign mercenaries, professional soldiers,
And Moors and worse than Moors,
But by men who passionately believed
In the cause for which they fought,—
Has stamped all the men I know,
The members of the International Brigade,
With a different bearing altogether
Than even the best, the most anti-militarist, gained
Of those who fought against Germany in the first Great War.
There in a man like Siegfried Sassoon, for example,
Despite the undeniable honesty, the little literary gift,
What is *Sherston's Progress* but an exposure
Of the eternal Englishman
Incapable of rising above himself,
And traditional values winning out
Over an attempted independence of mind?

Second-Lieutenant George Sherston went on strike against the war.
But his pacifism led him, not before a court-martial,
But into a hospital for the 'shell-shocked'.
There a psychiatrist, as clever as calm,
Coupled with plenty of good food and golf,
Restores Sherston to sanity.
He decided finally to return to the front,
Did so, found the job not too awfully awful, don't you know.
Was wounded, and ended up
In a rather nobler type of hospital
Where members of the royal family stopped by his bed
To offer forty-five seconds of polite sympathy.
And there the narrative ends, with Sherston as muddled as ever,

And given to rather vague—and glib—interrogations
That may be taken to express
His partial dissatisfaction with the universe.
As a transcript of a young man's actual emotions in war
The book is convincing enough. You must, however, regard
The young man as extremely average,
With no real self-knowledge
And no fixed scale of values.
He is anybody who has seen the blood and horror of war,
Which is a great deal less than we are supposed
To take Sherston to have been. Furthermore,
Seeing that almost twenty years lie
Between Sherston's experiences
And the writing of them down,
One looks for a sense of perspective,
A revision of values, a growth of understanding,
One nowhere encounters.
This is what happened to Sherston,
And so far as the book is concerned
Nothing ever happened afterwards.
There is possibly an argument in favour
Of presenting things simply as they were,
Of leaving them inclosed
Within their own time and place,
Without hindsight, without revaluation;
Though it is not easy to put it forward here,
Since the Sherston of today constantly and pointedly
Keeps interjecting himself into the picture.
But what is really wrong with the book
Is the portrait of Sherston as he then was:
A man so quickly able to accommodate himself,
After one flare of defiance,
To prevailing sentiment.
It is not that Sherston was either
A weak or a cowardly person.
It is rather that his rebelliousness was only
Superimposed on his profoundly English nature.
It would be unfair to say that, after coming out
Against war and all it signified,
He traduced his principles. Rather he changed his mind,
Regained the national disease of 'seeing things through,'
Saw them through, and ended up, pleased
That the royal family should stand by his hospital bed
And confer its verbal largesse. In other words

Sherston rebelled under stress of feeling,
Then conformed again under stress of feeling;
Throughout the ordeal he was altogether
The victim of his emotions.

This is not the stuff the members
Of the International Brigade were made of.
This is not enough to create, for me,
A provocative book.
Set against any of the better narratives of the war
By Continental writers, *Sherston's Progress* seems
Not only confused, but confused
In an immature and childish way.
In Mr Sassoon's book there is simply no evidence
Of a thinking mind; there is neither
Psychological nor philosophical substance.
There is only a young man who lets himself in
For a bad quarter of an hour and then,
Not because he lacks courage,
But because he lacks conviction,
Falls back into the ranks.
His real interests are golf,
Chasing the fox, reading poetry;
Is it too cynical to think at times
That his real objection to the war
Is its interfering with these pleasures?

But the members of the International Brigade
Were made of different stuff,
And will never fall back into the ranks.
And the war in Spain—and everywhere else—
Will never end till they win it,
Since they fight for Spain and not
        Just for castles in Spain.

51

THE TASK

Ah, Joyce, this is our task,
Making what a moving, thrilling, mystical, tropical,
Maniacal, magical creation of all these oppositions,
Of good to evil, greed to self-sacrifice,
Selfishness to selflessness, of this all-pervading atmosphere,
Of the seen merging with the unseen,
Of the beautiful sacrificed to the ugly,
Of the ugly transformed to the beautiful,
Of this intricate yet always lucid and clear-sighted
Agglomeration of passions, manias, occult influences,
Historical and classical references
—Sombre, insane, brilliant and sane,
Timeless, a symbol of the reality
That lies beyond and through the apparent,
Written with the sweeping assurance, the inspired beauty,
The intimated truth of genius,
With natures like ours in which a magnetic fluidity
That is neither 'good' nor 'bad' is forever
Taking new shapes under the pressure of circumstances,
Taking new shapes, and then again,
As Kwang makes Confucius complain of Laotze,
'Shooting up like a dragon.'
But, taking my life as a whole,
And hovering with the flight of the hawk
Over its variegated landscape,
I believe I detect certain quite definite 'streams of tendency'
In that unrolling map,
Moving towards the unknown future.
For one thing I fancy the manner I have allowed
My natural impulses towards romance and mysticism
To dominate me has led to the formation
Of a curious gap or 'lacuna'
Between the innate and almost savage realism,
Which is a major element in my nature,
And the imaginative, poetical cult
Whereby I have romanticised and idealised my life.
In this realistic mood I recognise
With a grim animal acceptance
That it is indeed likely enough that the 'soul'
Perishes everlastingly with the death of the body,

But what this realistic mood, into which
My mind falls like a plummet
Through the neutral zone of its balanced doubt,
Never for one single beat of time can shake or disturb
Is my certain knowledge,
Derived from the complex vision of everything in me,
That the whole astronomical universe, however illimitable,
Is only one part and parcel of the mystery of Life;
Of this I am as certain as I am certain that I am I.
The astronomical universe is *not* all there is.

So this is what our lives have been given to find,
A language that can serve our purposes,
A marvellous lucidity, a quality of fiery aery light,
Flowing like clear water, flying like a bird,
Burning like a sunlit landscape.
Conveying with a positively Godlike assurance,
Swiftly, shiningly, exactly, what we want to convey.
This use of words, this peculiar aptness and handiness,
Adapts itself to our every mood, now pathetic, now ironic,
Now full of love, of indignation, of sensuality, of glamour,
of glory,
With an inevitable richness of remembered detail
And a richness of imagery that is never cloying,
A curious and indescribable quality
Of sensual sensitiveness,
Of very light and very air itself,
—Pliant as a young hazel wand,
Certain as a gull's wings,
Lucid as a mountain stream,
Expressive as the eyes of a woman in the presence of love,—
Expressing the complex vision of everything in one,
Suffering all impressions, all experience, all doctrines
To pass through and taking what seems valuable from each,
No matter in however many directions
These essences seem to lead.

Collecting up all these essences,
These intimations coming willy-nilly from all quarters,
Into a complex conception of all things,
An intricately-cut gem-stone of a myriad facets
That is yet, miraculously, a whole;
Each of which facets serves its individual purpose
In directing the light collected from every side outwards

In a single creative ray.
With each of these many essences culled
From the vast field of life some part of one's own
Complex personality has affinity and resembles
When climbing on to the ice-cap a little south of Cape
  Bismarck
And keeping the nunataks of Dronning Louises Land on
  our left
We travel five days
On tolerable ice in good weather
With few bergs to surmount
And no crevasses to delay us.
Then suddenly our luck turns.
A wind of 120 miles an hour blows from the East,
And the plateau becomes a playground of gales
And the novel light gives us snow-blindness.
We fumble along with partially bandaged eyes
Our reindeer-skin kamiks worn into holes
And no fresh sedge-grass to stump them with.
We come on ice-fields like mammoth ploughlands
And mountainous séracs which would puzzle an Alpine
  climber.
That is what adventuring in dictionaries means,
All the abysses and altitudes of the mind of man.
Every test and trial of the spirit,
Among the debris of all past literature
And raw material of all the literature to be.

52

UTTERLY A CREATOR

The poetry of one the Russians call 'a broad nature'
And the Japanese call 'flower heart',
And we, in Scottish Gaeldom, '*ionraic*'
The poetry of one who practises his art
Not like a man who works that he may live
But as one who is bent on doing nothing but work,
Confident that he who lives does not work,
That one must die to life in order to be
Utterly a creator—refusing to sanction

The irresponsible lyricism in which sense impressions
Are employed to substitute ecstasy for information,
Knowing that feeling, warm heart-felt feeling,
Is always banal and futile.
Only the irritations and icy ecstasies
Of the artist's corrupted nervous system
Are artistic—the very gift of style, of form and expression,
Is nothing else than this cool and fastidious attitude
Towards humanity. The artist is happiest
With an idea which can become
All emotion, and an emotion all idea.
A poetry that takes its polish from a conflict
Between discipline at its most strenuous
And feeling at its highest—wherein abrasive surfaces
Are turned upon one another like millstones,
And instead of generating chaos
Refine the grist of experience between them.
The terrific and sustained impact
Of intellect upon passion and passion upon intellect,
Of art as a vital principle in the process
Of devising forms to contain itself,
Of germinal forces directed,
Not upon a void or an ego,
But upon living materials, in a way
That becomes physically oppressive
To almost everybody,
Recalling the figure of Aschenbach, 'whose greatest works
Were heaped up to greatness in layer after layer,
In long days of work, out of hundreds
And hundreds of single inspirations'.

53

THE GLASS OF PURE WATER

In the de-oxidisation and re-oxidisation of hydrogen in a single drop of water we have before us, truly, so far as force is concerned, an epitome of the whole life. . .The burning of coal to move an iron wheel differs only in detail, and not in essence, from the decomposition of a muscle to effect its own concentration.

James Hinton

We must remember that his analysis was done not intellectually, but by an immediate process of intuition; that he was able, as it were, to taste the hydrogen and oxygen in his glass of water.

Aldous Huxley (of D.H. Lawrence)

Praise of pure water is common in Gaelic poetry.

W.J. Watson: 'Bardachd Ghaidhlig'

Hold a glass of pure water to the eye of the sun!
It is difficult to tell the one from the other
Save by the tiny hardly visible trembling of the water.
This is the nearest analogy to the essence of human life
Which is even more difficult to see.
Dismiss anything you can see more easily;
It is not alive—it is not worth seeing.
There is a minute indescribable difference
Between one glass of pure water and another
With slightly different chemical constituents.
The difference between one human life and another
Is no greater; colour does not colour the water:
You cannot tell a white man's life from a black man's.
But the lives of these particular slum people
I am chiefly concerned with, like the lives of all
The world's poorest, remind me less
Of a glass of water held between my eyes and the sun
—They remind me of the feeling they had
Who saw Sacco and Vanzetti in the death cell
On the eve of their execution.
—One is talking to God.
I dreamt last night that I saw one of His angels
Making his centennial report to the Recording Angel
On the condition of human life.

Look at the ridge of skin between your thumb and
  forefinger.
Look at the delicate lines on it and how they change
—How many different things they can express—
As you move out or close in your forefinger and thumb.
And look at the changing shapes—the countless
Little gestures, little miracles of line—
Of your forefinger and thumb as you move them.
And remember how much a hand can express,
How a single slight movement of it can say more
Than millions of words—dropped hand, clenched fist.
Snapping fingers, thumb up, thumb down,
Raised in blessing, clutched in passion, begging,
Welcome, dismissal, prayer, applause,
And a million other signs, too slight, too subtle,
Too packed with meaning for words to describe,
A universal language understood by all.
And the Angel's report on human life
Was the subtlest movement—just like that—and no more;
A hundred years of life on the Earth
Summed up, not a detail missed or wrongly assessed,
In that little inconceivably intricate movement.

The only communication between man and man
That says anything worth hearing
—The hidden well-water; the finger of destiny—
Moves as that water, that angel, moved.
Truth is the rarest thing and life
The gentlest, most unobtrusive movement in the world.
I cannot speak to you of the poor people of all the world
But among the people in these nearest slums I know
This infinitesimal twinkling, this delicate play
Of tiny signs that not only say more
Than all speech, but all there is to say,
All there is to say and to know and to be.
There alone I seldom find anything else,
Each in himself or herself a dramatic whole,
An 'agon' whose validity is timeless.

Our duty is to free that water, to make these gestures,
To help humanity to shed all else,
All that stands between any life and the sun,
The quintessence of any life and the sun;

To still all sound save that talking to God;
To end all movements save movements like these.
India had that great opportunity centuries ago
And India lost it—and became a vast morass,
Where no water wins free; a monstrous jungle
Of useless movement; a babel
Of stupid voices, drowning the still small voice.
It is our turn now; the call is to the Celt.

This little country can overcome the whole world of
wrong
As the Lacedaemonians the armies of Persia.
Cornwall—Gaeldom—must stand for the ending
Of the essential immorality of any man controlling
Any other—for the ending of all Government
Since all Government is a monopoly of violence;
For the striking of this water out of the rock of Capitalism;
For the complete emergence from the pollution and fog
With which the hellish interests of private property
In land, machinery, and credit
Have corrupted and concealed from the sun,
From the gestures of truth, from the voice of God,
Hundreds upon hundreds of millions of men,
Denied the life and liberty to which they were born
And fobbed off with a horrible travesty instead
—Self-righteous, sunk in the belief that they are human,
When not a tenth of one per cent show a single gleam
Of the life that is in them under their accretions of filth.

And until that day comes every true man's place
Is to reject all else and be with the lowest,
The poorest—in the bottom of that deepest of wells
In which alone is truth; in which
Is truth only—truth that should shine like the sun,
With a monopoly of movement, and a sound like
talking to God. . . .

54

CRYSTALS LIKE BLOOD

I remember how, long ago, I found
Crystals like blood in a broken stone.

I picked up a broken chunk of bed-rock
And turned it this way and that,
It was heavier than one would have expected
From its size. One face was caked
With brown limestone. But the rest
Was a hard greenish-grey quartz-like stone
Faintly dappled with darker shadows,
And in this quartz ran veins and beads
Of bright magenta.

And I remember how later on I saw
How mercury is extracted from cinnabar
—The double ring of iron piledrivers
Like the multiple legs of a fantastically symmetrical spider
Rising and falling with monotonous precision,
Marching round in an endless circle
And pounding up and down with a tireless, thunderous force,
While, beyond, another conveyor drew the crumbled ore
From the bottom and raised it to an opening high
In the side of a gigantic grey-white kiln.

So I remember how mercury is got
When I contrast my living memory of you
And your dear body rotting here in the clay
—And feel once again released in me
The bright torrents of felicity, naturalness, and faith
My treadmill memory draws from you yet.

55

SONG OF THE SERAPHIM

Poverty is nothing but an outlived fettering
In the depths of the material regions
—In the mechanical, dead, inanimate
Or animal life of Nature.

This life we have now outgrown.
It lays the veil of the body over the spirit
And drags everything down to the level
Of a narrow materiality.

It is nothing but meanness and ugliness,
Stench, corruption, vice, decomposition, and dumbness.
The call is to intoxicated, burning lavishness.
Nothing now can bring poverty
Creatively to the front.
Poverty merely hinders the coming
Of the new Necessity
Which leads us to the End and Aim
Of our spirit and of the world,
Will make us steep and electric
And produce by force a new race
Of mariners on new and dangerous seas.

Poverty to-day desires nothing
But a material well-being
But the entire hopeless comfortlessness
Of a satisfied well-being
Must first be lived through,
Not merely described
Or held out to the poor
From afar.
The lower paradises
Must be outlived through satiety.
This is the call of the Seraphim.

Only he who hopes nothing more
From well-being and philistinism;
Only he who is no longer fettered
In the coarse material depths;
Only he who yearns for new needs

—The needs of the Heights
Not the needs of the Depths,
Immense and seraphic needs—
He only perceives
The impalpable and primordial life,
The Supreme—a life
Fuller, more real, and warmer
Than the chaotic deception
Of the palpable and objective
Which is apparently only effective
For everyday lower life.

To-day we are ripe to put an end
To poverty—to make an end
Of this necessity
For richness and abundance
In this world period
Become mankind.
But there is without doubt
Also a holy poverty,
A super-richness which falls to piece
In its own splendour,
A glowing love
That presses all fullness to itself,
Allows all small possessions to fall
More and more away from it,
All narrowness in relation
To things and to self—
Not from any ascetic discomfort,
But because of the poorness
Of these things in themselves.
Such is the glory
Of holy riches
And supreme prodigality.
The purpose of the old needs, therefore,
Cannot be 'well-being'
But only a new need.
Does the mighty proletarian assault
Of the poorest to-day desire nothing
But 'satiety', nothing but 'well-being'
With a smattering of art and education
Built philistine-wise upon it?

Does it not want as it asserts
To overcome the bourgeoisie,
But only to establish it forever
—Bourgeoisie itself in everything,
Not a step higher?
And that disgusts the few spiritual men,
But how can it disgust
Those poorest ones?
The deliverance of the proletariat cannot be
The affair of the proletariat itself,
As demagogic teaching declares.
It is in truth more than a sectional affair,
More than a class affair.

To-day something is beginning, as if the seed
Were losing itself in the bud.
Creation wants to-day to blossom
And raise itself to its topmost heights.
And if we wish to survive and not to suffocate,
Then in this day we must mount
An entirely new step higher, a greater step
Than that from the animal world
To the world of man.

That, however, is not technique,
Science, economics, organization, learning,
Or any kind of reform or 'cleverness'.
It is a *necessity* called for
By the eternal primordial life.
The new level of life does not depend
Upon a thing, nor upon
An individual.
It is an act of the never-ending creation,
Lying far beyond all individualist action.
Nevertheless we cannot mount
On to another plane of life
Until all the old possibilities,
Unto the very last,
Have been worn out and lived through.
For the way to the Supreme
Is in no way
The quickest and shortest.

It is a way most deeply sunk
And does not pass by
The smallest possibility of life,
For every part of the way
Is of equal value
In the Supreme. Every part
Is an aim in itself,
For the Supreme knows no 'Evolution'.

'Evolution' has only an entirely
'Inner-finite' significance.
It is a barbarous adoption,
As if somewhere, quite positive,
There were a Process—if possible, quite temporal—
Which in its issue, in its *sum*, determines the
'Essence' of the real;
Is itself absolute reality,
Universalness, the Supreme.
All our ideas about such a world process
Are nothing but a human and temporal view
And entirely adapted
To a temporal standard.

Every 'World Process' that we describe
Has only a world reality,
A reality of manifestation and technique.
We comprehend in it only
That which is objective and dead,
Never its life—for all life
Is incomprehensible.
Life is greater than all that can enter
Into the comprehensible.
Though I know all the limbs,
Entrails, organs, and functions of mankind,
Still am I as far as ever
From knowing 'man'
Who is more than the sum of his organs,
Which indeed only find
Their meaning and their life
When man's action precedes them.
We do not know a mosaic
By adding up the stones.
On the contrary,
The picture comes before the stones,
Without which the picture means nothing.

Whoever regards a 'World Process'
As a final reality
Is merely pursuing the anatomy
Of the corpse of all life.
This string of pearls, which in themselves
Are single and loose,
Is not the final form.
The world reality of such a process
In Thing, Individual, and Word
Is only its lowest form.

What we call *being* is only
The functioning of our consciousness,
Not the 'final Universal of All',
But the lowest.
It is the feeling, groping, consuming spirit;
Objective, matter-bound, but not living spirit.
That higher and stronger quickening life
We seek eternally and to-day
Must discover anew
Eternally transcends the objective spirit
Because it has nothing objective,
Only life.

But we draw the supreme Source of Life
Into the kingdom of Touch and Taste and Speech
If we signify it as something
'Behind' or 'Over' or 'Near',
Conformably to some spacious picture;
Or as the 'One', the 'Without Shape',
The 'Thing in Itself'. These are all
Materialistic, mediate things,
But 'the Supreme' and 'life' are immediate.
Pleroma is immediate, and is far away
Only from the gropers who seek
To muffle the infinite
In limitations and terms.
But to the high, crushing nearness
Of my exploding primordial life
The Supreme is 'that which is quite Nigh',
That which is without distance,
Immediateness itself, love-embrace,
The paradisiacal awareness
In which all fullness immediate and unredeemed,

Since all time, is posited timelessly,
Over 'Being', blessed in 'One'.
No empty abstraction, but the Life
Which can never be grasped,
That is transcendent.
And no bridge carries us
From 'Word' to 'trans',
Even as no bridge, but a leap,
Carries us from the plane to the cube,
From shallows to the bodily likeness.

56

THE INTERNATIONAL BRIGADE

Honour forever to the International Brigade!
They are a song in the blood of all true men.

The men of each nation showed qualities of their own.
The Swiss formidable for their dour obstinacy
And their concentrated, fretful impatience when not attacking;
The Poles kind-hearted, romantic, dashing and absolutely
fearless;
The English treat the war as a kind of job that has to be done
And they do it well (the pacifists from the English Universities
Make excellent machine-gunners). The Bulgarians
Have a preference for the hand-grenade. They resemble
The Spanish 'dynamiters' who storm machine-gun positions
With hand-made grenades. The French have the greatest number
Of deserters because it is easier for them
Than for any others both to come and go.
The French who remain are men of prodigious valour
And impetuosity. The Americans are an élite
By reason of their sober courage
And their simple keen intelligence.
The Germans are the best that Germany can give
(and that is saying much) many of them
Hardened by persecution and with much to avenge.

But if there had been a vote in the column
The Italians would have been shown as the favourites;
They combined a passionate chivalry and devotion
With supreme courage, resourcefulness, and discipline.
There can be no doubt at all that the Italian
Is a first-rate soldier when he is fighting
For a cause he has at heart.

The battle of Guadalajara brought face to face
Anti-Fascist Italians fighting
For an ideal to which they had dedicated their lives,
And Italians sent to Spain
To fight in a cause completely unknown to them.
Many of the latter had been deliberately tricked:
Signed on to be sent to Ethiopia
Where there would be work for them
And a livelihood for their families.
No interest of their country was at stake in Spain.
They had no reason to fight against the Spanish people,
Nor to shed their blood
For Spanish generals, bishops, and big landowners.
The alleged menace of Communism
Left them indifferent. What had they to lose
If Communism triumphed in Spain?
Or even in Italy? Wealth? They had none.
Liberty? They had none. To crown all
They found themselves fighting against Italians
Whose banner bore the name of Garibaldi
No wonder they listened to their fellow-countrymen
And refused to fight in a cause
Which could never be theirs.

No man worth calling a man can deny
The wonder and glory of the International Brigade.
They will live in history forever.
All the secrecy, sordidness, scheming and lying of the
Non-Interventionists
Was the fault of stuffy fools who are afraid of liberty.
The wide imaginative vision
Which touches the soul with the golden light of pity
Is hopelessly absent from every word they say.

How could they possibly understand such men?
Ideals of duty and sacrifice, firmly grasped,
And faithfully followed,

Led them to the starry heights where life
Becomes a divine adventure, and death
But an interlude leading
To yet more glorious achievement.

The soul of man became in them a dominant thing,
Its indestructibility in a world falling in ruins
Among scenes of indescribable horror
A thing to be held on to passionately.

They rang true. Is there more than one man
In a hundred thousand anywhere else
Of whom it is possible to say that
Courage and honesty
Are the foundations of his nature?

It is very rarely that a man loves
And when he does it is nearly always fatal.

The fire of life woke and burnt in these men
With that clear and passionate flame
That can only burn in those whose hearts are clean.
We were transported into the flaming heart of the world;
We stood in a place to which all roads came;
In a light which made all riddles clear.

Love and Pain, Terror and Ecstasy,
Strife and Fulfilment, Blasphemy and Prayer
Were one anothers' shadows,
Meeting and fading in a single radiance
That was not light nor heat,
But a movement, a flowing, that carried us along
And yet left us steadier,
More certain than we ever were before.

57

MAJOR ROAD AHEAD*

The workers of Spain have themselves become the Cid
Campeador.
A name whose original meaning is 'to be in the field,
The pasture.'
It has the further meanings of
'To frisk in the field,'
And so 'to be in the field of battle,'
And, especially, 'to be prominent in the field of battle,'
And so it came to mean 'surpassing in bravery'
And, in the mouths of their detractors,
'Men of the field, yokels.'
The word went from mouth to mouth among the timorous
Who had no better defence than their irony;
It slipped glibly from lips unctuous with envy.
'We are men of the field,' they cried,
Catching the jesting word like a ball hard driven,
Accepting the nickname with pride,
And launching it into the firmament,
And on their lips
The jesting word assumed a dignity
And sparkled and shone and flashed
And became a blazon and a star.

Who was the first to say it?
No man can tell. None of them knew.
It found itself suddenly upon all lips.
Was it born from the earth?
Did it fall from the sky,
From stones and trees,
From the dust and the air,
It was born from everywhere
At the same time,
It filled all space like light.

The heart of Spain expanded at the name
And embraced the world.
The name rose up,
Rose up into space,

* Written soon after the end of the Spanish Civil War.

Was charged and condensed
And fell again in a heroic rain.
A flight of swallows flying overhead
Caught up the name on the wing
And carried it to all the corners of the world.
The swallows sang it as they flew
And Spain grew by leagues
As it heard the name.

So their name issued suddenly
From all the pores of the earth,
And found itself upon all tongues,
Singing like a tree in the sun.
It was born and grew and ascended into Heaven,
Multiplied and was one with the forests,
Invaded the plains, crossed the mountains,
Covered Spain, leapt the frontiers and seas,
Filled all Europe,
Burst the boundaries of the world,
And grew and ascended,
And stayed only at Hope's zenith.

History and geography
Were obsessed with the name.
To the north, to the south,
To the east, to the west,
It was borne by the wind like a rose.
It passed above all banners and all birds
With a noise like a thousand banners,
A thousand birds,
While, beneath, a multitude
Weeping for joy,
Followed its passage on their knees
—Millions of heads
Raised in a branch of offering.
That heroic name is an eagle's nest
On the highest peak of History,
Sending through History a surge of song.
And there it remains through all eternity
Nestling on the strings of a lute.

You come to me shining from beyond the bourne of death,
You come to me across life,
Over a wide sea beneath a sky of doves.
The tide of the battle surges upon the gleaming shore of
your eyes.

Your eyes are two bas-reliefs of your glory.
Your hands are folded to offer up your heart.
Clothed in a comet,
You soar above Spain,
Above human history,
Into the infinite.

Your fury of love and faith
Planted four crosses to the wind
The garland of the four corners of the compass.
The hurricanes of God conjured you above your battles.
I saw you dedicate yourself
And arise out of your flesh
In a divine frenzy
Drawn up towards the infinite
In a mystic ecstasy,
A celestial drunkenness.

You are a tree which climbs and climbs
To bear up once more the Christ
Who came down to visit souls.
Bent over a flight of thunderbolts,
With your eyes fixed upon a journey,
Whither are you going?
In an immense sweep you soar resplendent
Up to the kingdom that is within yourself.
He who would now seek to follow the march of your
thoughts
Would lose his reason in dismay,
Would go astray in abysses of vertigo.
There are no limits to your soul.
Whither are you going?
How can I follow you?

The courses of the seven planets
Are reflected in the mirror of your shield.
Go your ways, go your ways,
Leave your flesh behind and go your ways

Clad in Epic.
I will watch beside you
As you roam the spaces of the stars
Without form and void,
As you circle the ellipse of God
I will keep vigil at the foot of your memory.
Your heart leaves a wake of spreading deeds
And perhaps I can follow you with my eyes.

They are gone.
Before my eyes
Their sword gleams and twists in a sudden blaze
And sprouts wings—two great wings of fire and
  flaming feather.

The sword moves, it is lifted up.
It soars, soars above my head, above the world.
I hear a hecatomb of planets falling into chaos.
I hear windows opening in space.
I hear eternity rushing in my ears.
Where am I? What is happening to me?
A whirlpool of light sucks me into its centre
And I fall down, down, down . . .

I have returned to earth,
To Spain.
I have come back to myself.

They were the people of destiny.
Of destiny, not fate.
Destiny went tied to their saddle-bow,
Linked with them in some mysterious fashion.
I do not know why.
In the presence of the fact
There is nothing to do
But bow the head.
As in a pack of cards
There is one ace of trumps,
So it is the habit of life;
Suddenly there emerges a man, a people,
Who is life's ace of trumps.

They were people of more than genius or than talent.
They were people of electricity.
Genius may fail of inspiration,
Talent may fail in calculation,
But the electric man
Does not fail in current.
Higher than the inspiration of genius
And a nicety of calculation
Is the discharge of a high potency,
The current of irresistible voltage,
Which a people can make pass
From one pole of the world to the other.

They were faith,
Ardour transfigured by faith,
The unconsciousness of faith,
The madness of faith which multiplies strength
And knows no possible barrier.
Wherever they passed there sprang behind their footprints
Mystic signs—I put it to the wisest
To reveal the mystery, to solve the problem.

The truth is that the problem has no solution.
They regarded themselves, they contemplated their work,
And they saw themselves escape from all laws
And enter into that region of the imponderable
Where things cannot be reduced to logic
So they were—and that was all about it.

Their bodies were a stupendous factory
Which manufactured the imponderable.
It was a factory
Which created the supernatural out of the natural,
Which created excess out of proportion,
Because all this factory worked
In the service of an exaltation
And this exaltation made them sublime
And made them illogical.

It was not logical that the Spanish workers should
 fight one against ten
Against World Fascism.—But so it was.
It was not logical that they should contend

Against superior numbers, superior armaments,
superior civilisation.
But it was so. And in the end
It will be seen that they have won,
And are consubstantial with all that has ever really lived
And lives forever as part and parcel
Of the very meaning and purpose of life.
An imperishable honour to Man;
One of the great glories of human life,
At the greatest turning point in human history
When mankind was faced at last with the sign:
MAJOR ROAD AHEAD.

The Battle continues.

For the spirit knows no compromise.

58

ON THE ASPORTATION OF THE SCONE STONE

Since David with a pebble in his sling
Goliath slew, now with this heavier stone
A little nation marks the opening
Of a like unequal battle for its own
And splits the atom of Earth's greatest throne.
This though perchance it prove like David's
fling
But 'juvenile delinquency' yet may bring
A like result—the giant overthrown!

Scotland knew better than to ask for bread
Merely to get (but took!) a stone instead,
England's stony response full well foreknown.
*Far more, O England, than the Scone stone's
gone,*
And all the King's horses and the King's men
Cannot set up your Humpty Dumpty again!

59

ON THE FLY-LEAF OF JEAN CASSOU'S *MASSACRES OF PARIS*

The shots of Gallifet did not truly kill Marie-Rose.
They pierced but one Marie-Rose.
Marie-Rose is immortal like her class,
A thousand times decimated, which carries
The standard of humanity into the light of the future.

Marie-Rose is the youth of this youth
Which I recommend to find its own reflection
In the story of the Commune, in the story of Spain,
And to draw from this reflection
A new lease of the enthusiasm
Which makes it unconquerable,
The enthusiasm of Gavroche and Vuillemin.

Thus the poet who is a true poet
Finds in the very life of the proletariat
The flame which transforms him, and which, in his turn,
By dint of his poet's gift, he renders back
To the class which incarnates all poetry,
The living animating poetry of struggle.

60

HIGH, LOW, JACK AND THE GODDAMN GAME

A poetry throwing light on the problems of value,
—Deriving its stimulating quality, its seminal efficacy,
Not from the discovery, as old as the Greeks,
That moral codes are relative to social factors,
But from the nice and detailed study of the mechanisms
Through which society
Determines attitudes in its members
By opening to them certain possibilities
By induction into objectively recognized statuses
While closing quite effectively other possibilities
—A poetry, not offering a compromise between naïve
atomism,

Giving an utterly unrelated picture of social phenomena,
And the unrealistic conception of a mystical social *Gestalt*,
The defining quality of which is intuited by transcendental
means
(That growing danger, as a reaction from the bankruptcy
Of the atomistic approach, of a mystical
Organismic approach instinct with anti-rationalist
obscurantism),
But seeking to do justice to the discrete
As well as to the organically integrated aspects of society,
To the disruptive as well as to the cohesive forces
—A poetry that men weary of the unscientific wrangling
Of contemporary social and political dogmatists
Will find a liberating experience
—Rich in its discoveries of new problems,
Important questions so far unsuspected,
For which field research does not yet apply
The data necessary to answer them.

A poetry that is—to use the terms of Red Dog*—
High, low, jack and the goddamn game.

61

FOR DANIEL COHN-BENDIT

(On the occasion of his candidature in Glasgow University Rectorial Election, 1968)†

No man or group of men has any right
To force another man or other groups of men
To do anything he or they do not wish to do.
There is no right to govern without
The consent of the governed. Consent is not only
Important in itself, and as a nidus for freedom
And its attendant spontaneity, (clearly valuable
As the opposed sense of frustration is detrimental)
But the sole

* Red Dog = American pastime.
† The author was one of Cohn-Bendit's sponsors on this occasion.

Basis of political obligation. There is nothing
Supplemental to or coequal with consent itself
And even if we had not the lessons of all history
—The endless evidence of 'man's inhumanity to man'
And overwhelming proof that all power debases
And that no man is good enough to have it
Or can exercise it without doing far more harm than good—
The contention is utterly indefensible—sheer humbug! mortmain!
That 'so long as the exercise of certain powers is good in itself
Or a means to the good . . . these powers are right
Whether or not anyone is of the opinion that they are,'
The time-dishonoured formula that attempts to conceal or excuse
All the hellish wrong of human history,
The fraud and loss inherent in all Government,
That age-long monstrous distortion of the faculties of man
It is the great historical task of the working-class
To eliminate today, no matter at what cost,
That human life, no longer wrenched hideously awry,
May spring up at last in its proper form.

62

OLD WIFE IN HIGH SPIRITS

In an Edinburgh Pub

An auld wumman cam' in, a mere rickle o' banes, in a faded
  black dress
And a bonnet wi' beads o' jet rattlin' on it;
A puir-lookin' cratur, you'd think she could haurdly ha'e
  had less
Life left in her and still lived, but dagonit!

He gied her a stiff whisky—she was nervous as a troot
And could haurdly haud the tumbler, puir cratur;
Syne he gied her anither, joked wi' her, and anither, and syne
Wild as the whisky up cam' her nature.

rickle o' banes, living skeleton   cratur, creature

The rod that struck water frae the rock in the desert
Was naething to the life that sprang oot o' her;
The dowie auld soul was twinklin' and fizzin' wi' fire;
You never saw ocht sae souple and kir.

Like a sackful o' monkeys she was, and her lauchin'
Loupit up whiles to incredible heights;
Wi' ane owre the eight her temper changed and her tongue
Flew juist as the forkt lichtnin' skites.

The heich skeich auld cat was fair in her element;
Wanton as a whirlwind, and shairly better that way
Than a' crippen thegeither wi' laneliness and cauld
Like a foretaste o' the graveyaird clay.

Some folk nae doot'll condemn gie'in' a guid spree
To the puir dune body and raither she endit her days
Like some auld tashed copy o' the Bible yin sees
On a street book-barrow's tipenny trays.

A' I ken is weel-fed and weel-put-on though they be
Ninety per cent o' respectable folk never hae
As muckle life in their creeshy carcases frae beginnin' to end
As kythed in that wild auld carline that day!

dowie, sad fizzing, blazing
souple, nimble kir, cheerful
loupit, leapt whiles, at times
skites, strikes heich, high
skeich, spirited fair, fully
shairly, surely crippen theither, huddled up
tipenny, twopenny muckle, much
creeshy, fat kythed, showed, appeared
carline, old woman

63

LAMH DEARG ABOO
(To Stalin)

Stalin, when we Scottish Gaels salute you
It is, like all else, by no mere chance
That an old battle-cry of our people at last
Wins on our lips to its full significance
—Lamh dearg aboo!*

Suddenly we know what one meant who cried
'Montrose fought for more than his king—he fought for all men.'
And see the underlying meanings of 1645
And 1745 leap up in us again
—Lamh dearg aboo!

We know now why our Gaeldom had to fall for a while
Under the English, Money, the Church and the Law
And see fully at last what our kin through the ages
Only at their best in fleeting glimpses saw.
—Lamh dearg aboo!

1645, 1745—and now in the midst
Of history's greatest and final war
We believe by 1945 the true sense
Of all our tangled tale will shine out like a star.
—Lamh dearg aboo!

Ah, Stalin, we Scots who had our first home
In Caucasian Georgia like yourself see how
The processes of history in their working out
Bring East and West together in general human triumph now.
—Lamh dearg aboo!

The very centre and lifeblood of Scotland is here,
Misprized and distorted for hundreds of years,
Now there fluent Gaelic sunshine floods through at last
And all the fog of oppression and cant disappears.
—Lamh dearg aboo!

* Battle-cry of the Scottish and Irish MacDonalds under Alasdair MacDonald and Montrose at Tippermuir, Inverlochy, etc. Means 'The Red Hand to Victory.'

Scottish history—ah, indeed, a strange woman,
Incomprehensible creature, full of faults to the brim,
And yet of a curious twisting tenderness! Scottish history—good?
Fools laugh —as some chucklehead might at one of the Seraphim.
 —Lamh dearg aboo!

'Ask your red-faced friend at Scotland Yard.
He has no illusions about me, I know.
Morally I am in the depths. But to you—to you,
What falls grey in London is still pure as Schiehallion's golden
 snow.'*
 —Lamh dearg aboo!

It is to-day as when Montrose and his men
Struggled up out of the bed of the Tarff through the night.
Came a shaft of red through the blackest clouds and suddenly
The whole vast scene took shape and colour round them, and
 bright,
Up behind the Monadhliath Mountains broke the dawn
—Not a Five Years' this, but a Millennium's plan.
 —Lamh dearg aboo!

Red and snow-white?† Have these startling colours
Ever flared in such high conjunction before?—Aye, so they
 sprang
When from the highest mountain in Britain's three kingdoms
Suddenly in the white and scarlet air Montrose's trumpets sang.
 —Lamh dearg aboo!

Fifteen hundred men and a body of horse
Without food and without rest for thirty-six hours
Scaling the inaccessible mountains of Lochaber in midwinter!
—So all the meaning of our history suddenly flowers.
 —Lamh dearg aboo!

Away with the word 'impossible'. Here surely
Was no trip for anyone not of the bird clan.
Bifrost Bridge, sharp as a sword-edge, which stretches to
 Valhalla?
Straiter still is the way of all true greatness in man!
 —Lamh dearg aboo!

* Golden snow, i.e. snow in sunlight. Pindar's phrase.
† The poet is coupling here the Red Flag of Russia and Scotland's Silver Saltire.

To see this is as when in a great ship's engine-room
Through all the vastness of furnaces and clanging machinery
  is found
The quiet simple thing all that is about—a smooth column of
  steel,
The propeller shaft, in cool and comfortable bearings, turning
  round and round with no sound
—All the varying forces, the stresses and resistances,
Proceeding from that welter of machinery.
Unified into the simple rotation of this horizontal column,
And conducted calmly along its length into the sea.
    —Lamh dearg aboo!

64

A SPRIG OF WHITE HEATHER IN THE FUTURE'S LAPEL

'Jesus, he's got it. He's got whatever
that thing called charisma is. He's sure,
He's confident. He's got presence.'

For Willie Gallacher's eightieth birthday celebrations arranged by the Scottish Committee of the Communist Party of Great Britain in St Andrew's Halls, Glasgow, on Sunday 24 December 1961, I wrote a poem entitled 'Scottish Universal'. That title was the name of the combined business enterprises of a Glasgow millionaire, Sir Hugh Fraser, but I made it clear at once that I was not writing about these, but about something truly entitled to the name, the life-work of Willie Gallacher. And in the poem I said of him:

One of the few decent politicians in Britain today!
That does not prevent a man having enemies.
On the contrary, the more unswervingly upright—
The more powerful the hatred he arouses,
The deadlier the enmity combining against him.

So we have had it here—a man indefatigable
In his attention to affairs, serving his constituents
With sustained ability and scrupulous devotion,
A genial man, exemplary citizen, and loving husband.
Not many men tested in the acrid fires
Of public life come through so intact and unsullied,
Pure gold thrice refined. I remember as a boy
Scarching a wide Border moor, acres of purple heather.
Looking for white heather—and suddenly
I saw it, hundreds of yards away,
Unmistakable—so in the hosts of men I've known
Willie Gallacher shines out, single of purpose,
Lovely in his integrity, exemplifying
All that is best in public service—distinct,
Clear-headed and clean-hearted,
A great humanist, true comrade and friend,
Without variableness or shadow of turning,
Eighty years young in his sterling spirit
And the immaculate courage of his convictions.

A sprig of white heather in the future's lapel.
A wave and cheerful handshake for all mankind!
But surely he has some fault? Yes, of course,
The worst of all, the unforgivable knack of being always right.

65

THE SKELETON OF THE FUTURE
(At Lenin's Tomb)

Red granite and black diorite, with the blue
Of the labradorite crystals gleaming like precious
  stones
In the light reflected from the snow; and behind them
The eternal lightning of Lenin's bones.

66

THE STORM-COCK'S SONG

My song today is the storm-cock's song.
When the cold winds blow and the driving snow
Hides the tree-tops, only his song rings out
In the lulls in the storm. So let mine go!

On the topmost twig of a leafless ash
He sits bolt upright against the sky
Surveying the white fields and the leafless woods
And distant red in the East with his buoyant eye.

Surely he has little enough cause to sing
When even the hedgerow berries are already pulped by
  the frost
Or eaten by other birds—yet alone and aloft
To another hungry day his greeting is tossed.

Blessed are those who have songs to sing
When others are silent; poor song though it be,
Just a message to the silence that someone is still
Alive and glad, though on a naked tree.

What if it is only a few churning notes
Flung out in a loud and artless way?
His 'Will I do it? Do it I will!' is worth a lot
When the rest have nothing at all to say.

67

MY SONGS ARE KANDYM IN THE WASTE LAND

Above all, I curse and strive to combat
The leper pearl of Capitalist culture
Which only tarnishes what it cannot lend
Its own superb lustre.

Somewhere in its creative faculty is concealed
A flaw, a senseless and wanton quality
That has no human answer.
An infernal void.

Capitalist culture to the great masses of mankind
Is like the exploitative handling in America
Of forest, grazing, and tilled lands
Which exaggerates floods and reduces
The dry-season flow of the rivers to almost nothing.

A hundred million acres, which might have maintained
A million families, utterly destroyed by water erosion,
Nine million acres destroyed by wind,
Hundreds of millions of acres more
Yielding rapidly to wind and water erosion,
Forests slashed to the quick
And the ground burned over,
Grazing lands turned into desert,
The tragic upsetting of the hydrologic cycle
Which has turned into disastrous run-off
The water that should have been held in the soil
To support vegetation and percolate
To the lower levels and feed wells and springs,
Till now the levee builders try to raise
The Mississippi and set it up on stilts
Whence sooner or later it must stumble.

Problems of erosion control, regulation of river-flow,
Flood control, silt control, hydro-electric power.
I turn from this appalling spectacle
Of illimitable waste; and set myself, they say,
Gad im ghainimh (putting a withy round sand).
The sand will produce a vegetation itself
If it is not interfered with. It will be a slow growth.
Nevertheless the vegetation manages to get a start
In the course of thousands of years,
And my poetry will be like the kandym
That doesn't advance step by step
But goes forward on the run, jumps through the air,
The little nut jumps along like a ball,
The sand comes along after, but the sand is heavier
And cannot catch up with the little nut
And bury it. But when the seed takes root
And the little shrub starts, the shrub
Cannot jump along like the seed ball.

How is it going to save itself
From the encroaching waves of sand?
It is not so easy to bury the kandym.
It doesn't have branches like those
Of the apricot and peach tree—its branches
Are slender and there are no leaves on them.
When the sand comes on the kandym doesn't try to stop it
But lets it go right through its branches,
Gives it right-of-way.

But sometimes the sand waves are so big
They bury the kandym nevertheless.
Then a race begins—the dune grows and the plant grows.
The dune grows fast but the plant grows faster still
And by the time the sand dune has attained its final height
The plant is found to have outstripped it.
Its little green bristles are waving in the wind
On the crest of the sand dune.
It has not only grown in height but has branched out too.
The whole dune is perforated with its branches.
The wave passes on, leaving behind
A good half of its sand.
So the little kandym has stopped the advance of the sand,
Turned the dune into a little hillock
Covered with vegetation.

But is there not one last danger?
The wind may blow the sand away
And leave the roots bare?
But the kandym knows how to fight with the wind too.
Lying flat on the sand it sends out extra roots
And holds the sand down with them.
In this way it gathers up the soil
And makes a foothold for itself.

My songs are kandym in the Waste Land.

INDEX OF FIRST LINES